Strange Communists I Have Known

What attracted some extraordinarily gifted men and women to communism and then led them to reject it?

Here, one of the most respected historians and biographers of our time presents portraits of ten gifted people who were involved in the communist movement, served it, then broke with it.

"Those who streamed towards Moscow," says Wolfe, "were a variegated band, each unique in his person. For a shorter or longer time they seemed to adapt themselves, repeat the same phrases, obey the same orders, be shaped, or silenced, into an appearance of conformity to the blueprint. Then as they questioned or rebelled or measured the dream against the deed, they broke away, each in his own fashion and for his own reasons, and suddenly, startlingly, they assumed their own human shape once more."

Here is a work reminiscent of, yet superior to, *The God That Failed.*

BY *Bertram D. Wolfe*

Strange Communists I Have Known

90-097

A SCARBOROUGH BOOK
STEIN AND DAY/*Publishers*/New York

To the strangest of them all,
this book is affectionately dedicated.

ACKNOWLEDGMENTS   Portions of text in some chapters, revised for
inclusion in the present work, appeared previously in the following publications: *American Heritage; The New Leader;* the author's introduction to
Impressions of Lenin by Angelica Balabanoff (University of Michigan
Press); his introduction to *The Russian Revolution and Leninism or Marxism?* by Rosa Luxemburg (University of Michigan Press); *Slavic Review;
Commentary;* and the author's *Three Who Made a Revolution* (Dial Press).

FIRST SCARBOROUGH BOOKS EDITION 1982

Strange Communists I Have Known was originally published in hardcover by Stein
and Day/*Publishers.*

Designed by David Miller
Printed in the United States of America
Stein and Day/*Publishers*
Scarborough House
Briarcliff Manor, N.Y. 10510
ISBN 0-8128-6120-5

Contents

Illustrations

Introduction

THIS IS A gallery of ten portraits of colorful and adventurous men and women I have known. The five who appear in Part I, I knew through personal friendship: John Reed, Jim Larkin, Sam Putnam, Angelica Balabanoff, Yusuf Meherally. The five, each in his own way, was attracted to the communist movement, sought to serve it loyally, then broke with it. They are a varied company —a poet; a devout Catholic Irish labor leader; a critic; a warm-hearted, sentimental woman who yearned to serve the poor and give their lives more dignity; an Indian socialist, one-time Mayor of Bombay, who insisted on bringing the communists of India into his party and into the Indian National Congress, then expelled them to the last man when he found that there was no place for moral principle in their politics. Since these five were my friends, it is only fair to put the reader on notice that my view of them may be colored by the affection and charity that go with friendship. Yet I am not one who believes that love is blind. On the contrary, it may see qualities in the object of its affection that indifferent eyes fail to notice. In any case, friendship has moved me to try to keep their memories green and to explain the reasons that brought these five gentle human beings to a movement that has so little that is gentle in it.

The other five in this gallery of portraits, those appearing in Part II, are men and women whom I have

known principally by a different mode of knowledge,
namely that of historical research. Their "strangeness," too,
as communists, is of quite another character. Since they
lived much of their lives in the underground, the research
of the historian has had to be supplemented by considerable detective work. Indeed, the final sketch in this book
is a genuine detective story in which I set out to find for
the publishing house of Harper and Brothers (now Harper
and Row) whether Maxim Litvinov, the well-known Bolshevik leader and Soviet Foreign Commissar, was the real
author of a manuscript offered them as *The Litvinov
Diary*, and I ended with some insight into the character
and life of the man who fabricated the "Diary," himself
a veteran of the Soviet Foreign Service.

The case of the "Double Agent" is also a true detective story calling for investigation on many levels, for
Roman Malinovsky turned out to be a police agent in the
very top of Lenin's inner circle, the leader of Lenin's trade
union, parliamentary, and domestic underground work,
and a man whose double role in the end so confused him
that he was no longer altogether sure whether he was
Lenin's agent in the police or the agent of the police in
Lenin's underground.

Two of the three women in this book, Rosa Luxemburg and Inessa Armand, also required investigation beyond the normal range of historical research. The true
outlines of Rosa Luxemburg's spirit and life were obscured
by a subsequent legend portraying her as a leading col-
laborator of Lenin's in Germany, Poland, Russia, and the
Comintern. Actually, though she accounted herself, like
him, a revolutionary socialist, she fought tenaciously all
her life against his characteristic views on organization,
terror, morality, military discipline, and dictatorship, and
with her last breath instructed her delegate to Moscow
to oppose the founding of the Comintern in 1919.

As to the relations between Lenin and Inessa Armand,
that piece of literary detective work hit the headlines first

in *Izvestia,* then in all the leading newspapers of the West, when the Soviet Government ousted the *Time* correspondent and closed the *Time* Bureau in Moscow because that magazine had ventured to devote a single sentence to summarizing the article I wrote for a scholarly journal, *The Slavic Review,* on "Lenin and Inessa Armand." It, too, is a true detective story.

Though Jim Larkin was twenty years older than I, Angelica Balabanoff eighteen years older, John Reed nine, and Sam Putnam four, we all thought of each other as contemporaries. That feeling had nothing to do with chronological age but was connected with two crucial years and an overpowering experience that gave to our lives for years a common mood and the spin of a common trajectory.

For the older men and women in this gallery of portraits, the year 1914 marked the end of a world. And for young and old alike, for me, then only twenty-one, and even, retrospectively, for Yusuf Meherally who was ten years my junior, the year 1917 was the beginning of a new world. One cannot understand what these so diverse personalities had in common or felt in common unless one bears in mind the overpowering influence of those two decisive dates, 1914 and 1917, on the history of our times.

The year 1914 marked the beginning of a Time of Troubles that continues to the present day. On August 1 of that year began the first total war, followed by the first false peace, a peace made up of lesser wars and major and minor revolutions, which built up into World War II. And, looking at the nature of the peace that is no peace today, who can say that the Time of Troubles is over?

On that summer night in 1914 when Sir Edward Grey, looking out of his Chancellery window at the lowering night, sadly prophesied: "The lights are going out all over Europe never to be rekindled again in our generation," even he could not foresee that the dark would last into the present half of the century. Somehow we have gotten used to it. But the men and women in these pages were of the generation that stumbled from the light into the sudden darkness, and, shocked at that darkness, rebelled against the world that had thus revealed a crisis in its very foundations.

What was blacking out that night was the grand century of peace and progress that began when Napoleon fell in 1815 and ended when peace fell in 1914, a century optimistic and sure of itself, certain of the inevitable onward and upward march of civilization.

Ending that night was the dream that the modern world was "too civilized for war." With it ended many other dreams to which the eighteenth century had given such rational form and the nineteenth had seemed to make so much progress in realizing: dreams of cosmopolitanism and internationalism; of the abolition of poverty in an economy of abundance; of the free movement of men, ideas, and goods in an ever more open society; dreams of a limited state increasingly controlled from below, and with ever surer curbs on autocratic and dictatorial power; of gentler and juster laws, the abolition of all forms of involuntary servitude and of capital punishment for crimes against property; dreams of liberty, equality, and brotherhood, and the creation of a new man, free in spirit and intelligence, free in critical inquiry, master to an ever greater extent of nature, his own nature, and his institutions. It was the shipwreck of these dreams that brought the men and women here portrayed to a movement that did not scruple to trade on the dreams but has proved to be the very negation of their essence.

Until August, 1914, Adolf Hitler was a lonely crackpot crawling among other lonely crackpots on the outer margins of society, and Lenin was a rejected pedant of total organization, conspiracy, and terror, buried ever deeper in a disintegrating underground. But then began four long, terrible years during which generals and statesmen treated their people as human material to be expended without stint or calculation in the pursuit of undefined and un-attainable goals—tens of thousands of men to gain a few hundred yards of muddy ground, and then an even larger number to lose the same few yards again.

Men learned to master their fear of death and their revulsion at inflicting it. Universal war so brutalized civil-ized man that it became possible to beguile him into fresh brutalities by the fury of his resentment against brutality. Since it was a time of horrors, men said, at least let violence have peace as its objective and as its enemy the civilization and the leaders that had made the carnage possible. Before there could come the reign of what Churchill called "the bloody-minded professors of the Kremlin," there first had to be the bloody mess of Flanders Field, where, as Eng-land's war-time leader, Lloyd George, wrote, "Nothing could stop Haig's compulsion to send thousands and thousands to their death against the enemy's guns in the bovine and brutal game of attrition."

The year 1917 brought the first apparent rift in the darkness. It was the year in which Russia left the war just as America was entering it.

"Comrade Machine Gun has the floor," wrote the communist poet, Mayakovsky. The age of violence and the bloody trenches where armies held their ground yet de-stroyed each other were Lenin's (as they were to be Hitler's) opportunity.

It was the refusal of raw reserve units of peasants-in-uniform in the Capital to obey their officers that brought the Tsar down in the spring, a downfall which was totally unexpected to Lenin. And it was the failure of the same peasants-in-uniform to defend the new, free institutions of democratic Russia in the fall of 1917 that enabled Lenin and his tiny band of conspirators to seize the strong points of the city, overthrow what Lenin himself described as "the freest government in the world," and set up in its place his own permanent and total dictatorship.

"The age of discussion ends," wrote Spengler expressing the new mood, "and the age of 'election as revolution in legitimate forms' yields to one in which mankind 'elects' its Destiny again by the primitive methods of bloody violence. . . . The dice are there, ready for this stupendous game. Who dares to throw them?" Lenin dared, and won. The persuasiveness of success added to the persuasiveness of power made it seem to many that he had been right in everything all along.

"To seize power," he had written on the eve of the seizure, "is the point of the uprising; afterwards we will see what we can do with it." Lenin was too taken with his new-found power to jeopardize it by trying to carry out at once his avowed purpose, namely, to use it to continue the war, turning it from an "imperialist war" into a universal civil war.

The peasant-in-uniform had voted for peace "with his feet," and Lenin needed the support of the armed peasantry, or at least its neutrality, while he established his dictatorship over Russia. "What was the main thing in 1917?" he asked his followers rhetorically at the Eleventh Congress of his party. "It was emerging from the war, which the entire people demanded . . . and this gave us victory for many years. . . . Whatever stupidities and outrageous things we did in other fields, once we had taken this task into account, it signified [to the masses] that everything was all right."

From all lands men and women turned in the midst of the darkness of universal war towards the beacon of hope they thought they saw shining from the towers of the Kremlin. Men who hated war and longed for peace turned towards the false dawn in the East because they had been shocked to their inmost depths by the failure of all their institutions, from the churches of the Prince of Peace to the socialist international.

Socialists looked towards Moscow for the redemption of the sullied honor of their movement. Impatient rebels, who had long fretted at the slowness with which the nineteenth century had been realizing their dreams and were now shocked by the speed with which the civilized world had relapsed into brutality, thought that Lenin's success represented a short cut to the realization of those dreams. In his first decree, Lenin called to the world simultaneously for peace and world revolution. For him the call for peace was a means to bring about revolution, but many heard it as a call for revolution to bring about peace.

The first pilgrims to the new Mecca, such as John Reed, Angelica Balabanoff, and Jim Larkin, saw the beacon through the mists of their own illusions. From all the ends of the earth, across mountains and seas, through shell-torn battlefields, and past unsleeping sentries, they found their way to answer Lenin's call. Each heard what he longed to hear; each managed to be deaf to that which meant most to Lenin, but did not fit his own dreams.

The lives of those who survived the first terrible years of disillusion tell a hopeful story. Almost as soon as they arrived, Lenin began his struggle to reshape their spirits according to his blueprint of ruthlessness, amoralism, and unthinking obedience, and to replace their love and pity for their fellowmen by hatred for "the system" and the men that in his mind embodied it. Lenin saw his followers as will-less cogs in his machine. For a time it seemed as if he might really turn this variegated band of rebels and dreamers into something like identical cogs in a machine, or ball-bearings of equal diameter and hardness to support the shaft of his juggernaut.

But human beings are infinite in their variety and the human spirit is a stubborn thing. Those who streamed towards Moscow were even more varied than ordinary men, each high spirited and unique in his own person. For

a shorter or longer time they strove to preserve their illusions. They seemed to adapt themselves, repeat the same
phrases, obey the same orders, be shaped, or silenced, into
an appearance of conformity to Lenin's blueprint. But one
by one they questioned, measured the dream against the
deed, rebelled, then broke away, each for his own reasons
and in his own fashion. Suddenly, startlingly, they assumed
their original human shapes once more. They were profoundly changed by this experience to be sure, but each
changed in ways that accorded with his own nature and
intensified its original qualities. The very colors that were
to have been bleached out were the aspects of their spirits
which the experience reinforced.

> BERTRAM D. WOLFE
> The Hoover Institution for the
> Study of War, Revolution and Peace,
> Stanford, Spring, 1965

PART ONE

1

The Harvard Man in the Kremlin Wall

JOHN REED was as American as apple pie and store cheese. Yet he was one of the founders of the Communist International, and his ashes lie under the Kremlin wall. From a mansion on Cedar Hill in Portland, Oregon, through respectable Harvard College, to the Kremlin wall in the heart of Moscow—such is the trajectory of his life. Except that his further evolution was cut short by untimely death, it was the trajectory, too, of the pre-1914 Greenwich Village radicalism of which he was an integral part. Indeed, to follow his adventures of flesh and spirit is to learn more about native American radicalism than about Russian communism.

John Silas Reed, as he was christened in Portland's fashionable Trinity Episcopal Church, was born on October 20, 1887, in the sumptuous mansion of his maternal grandparents. His childhood memories center around their lordly hilltop home, "a French chateau, with immense park, formal gardens, lawns, stables, greenhouses, glass grape-arbor, tame deer . . . Chinese servants . . . idols,

23

strange customs and ceremonies . . . pig-tails and gongs and fluttering red paper."

But Jack's father and mother, the C. J. Reeds, were neither so rich nor so colorful. They owned a little home in Portland, then moved to an apartment hotel. His father did well as agent for an eastern agricultural implement company until the International Harvester trust swallowed it up. Then he struggled along as an insurance salesman. He strove to give his two sons the education proper to Portland "society" (private school, eastern prep school, Harvard), never letting his boys know the effort it cost him. In later years he became a crusader against the deeds of the great Portland families of which his father-in-law was a leading representative. Some of Oregon's leaders were pre-empting the forests (to say Oregon was to say lumber). When Theodore Roosevelt began his battle for conservation of the forest lands, C. J. Reed became a United States marshal to fight the despoilers of the Oregon forests. The divisions in Portland society, the excitements of the crusade, the friendship between Jack's father and Lincoln Steffens, the firing of Portland's United States marshal by Taft—such was the political heritage which John Reed took with him to Harvard and Greenwich Village.

Jack's boyhood was troubled by illness, particularly a kidney ailment, a sense of physical weakness, the fear of older and tougher boys. He was never really well and strong until his sixteenth year. His way to the Portland Academy lay through Goose Hollow, inhabited by "brutal Irish boys." He fought when he had to, ran when he could, paid tribute to his tormenters, finally got himself accepted precariously as one of the less valued members of the Fourteenth Street Gang.

The boy's happiness was not in the world of fights and sports but, his mother having early taught him to read, in the world of books and dreams. Soon he was writing verses, telling fanciful tales to younger listeners, seeing in every girl a Guinevere and in himself Sir Galahad, aquest for the Holy Grail. "History was my passion, kings strutting about and armored ranks of men." Much later, when he had reached the age of twenty-six and had gotten to Florence, he thought he saw a "Field of Dragons' Teeth, where turbulent armies bred"; and in Venice he was lost in the beauty of history. "The things *men* have done!" he murmured over and over again to Mabel Dodge. "But I wish that *I* could have been there at the *doing* of it, or that they were doing it *now*."

But in the Portland Academy of his boyhood, Jack was an outsider. "I wasn't good at the things the other boys were, and their codes of honor and conduct didn't hold me . . . They had a good natured contempt for me . . . That is why my impression of my boyhood is an unhappy one, and why I have so few close friends in Portland, and don't ever want to live there again."

Only at swimming did he excel, spending long hours in the Willamette River outdiving and outracing his companions. He staged plays of his own writing, founded and managed juvenile journals, filling them with his own stuff. Since his education was what is today called "permissive," and his reading wide and disorderly, his mind would be to the end as amazing for what he didn't know as for what he did, and most amazing for the things he knew that weren't so. In 1917, just before he left for his look at the Russian Revolution, he wrote a brief memoir, a backward glance at the first twenty-nine years of his life, from which I have been quoting. Of the temper of his spirit he wrote:

> I never stuck long at anything I didn't like . . . On the other hand, there are few things I don't get some fun out of, if only the novelty of experience. I love people, except the well-fed smug, and am interested in all new things and all the beautiful old things they do. I love beauty and chance and change . . . I suppose I'll always be a Romanticist.

No one could put better what his friends meant when they said: "Jack is a poet."

Obsessed with the sense of being an outsider, his youth was absorbed with an attempt to belong. In the eastern prep school to which his family sent him to prepare for Harvard, he was more successful. His health better, though his kidney never ceased to give trouble, he played football and ran the quarter mile. Where all were strangers, they were more willing to accept him.

But in Harvard, which he entered in 1906, he felt an outsider once more. Of the 744 young men in his entering class, it seemed that all had friends but Jack. How to make acquaintances, get into the clubs, become a part of all the gaiety? To make the freshman crew he stayed all through a lonely vacation in Cambridge practicing on the rowing machine, only to be the last man dropped from the squad before the meets began. He tried out for the college papers, sought a desirable roommate and was snubbed, snubbed a Jewish boy who wanted to room with him—for which he sought and won forgiveness later. Through it all, he felt terribly alone.

As an upperclassman, his status improved. He made one of the papers as managing editor, though the top posts eluded him "because the aristocrats blackballed me." He had actually prayed to God to make his fellow students like him; now his prayers were being fulfilled. To be sure, he never made the "better" clubs, except Hasty Pudding in his senior year, when it needed someone to compose comic lyrics for the annual show. But he became president of the Cosmopolitan Club, outsiders banded together from forty-three lands, which offered the boy from Portland a heady brew of ideas and ideologies. Administrative posts were open to him: manager of the Dramatic Club, manager of the musical clubs, captain of the water polo team (recognition for his long hours of swimming in the Willamette), song leader of Harvard's cheering section, where "I had the blissful sensation of swaying two thousand voices in great crashing choruses during the big football games." His admiration for Bill Nye and Mark Twain, and his fecundity in thinking up sophomoric jokes and comic rhymes, won him second place on the *Lampoon*. He got on the *Monthly*, but could not make the staff of *The Crimson*, the Harvard daily. He felt almost, but not quite, "in."

When a fight developed between "aristocrats" and "commoners," Reed wavered. The commoners lived in the dormitories in Harvard Yard, the aristocrats on Mt. Auburn Street, whence the fight was known as one between Yard and Street. Tempted by the symbols of status, Jack had taken a room on the Street. That, and a modicum of acceptance from the "insiders" in his senior year, made him choose to run on their ticket—and go down to defeat.

Even then, the aristocrats did not altogether accept him. When he did get invited to their Back Bay drawing rooms, a perverse, defiant streak made him play some prank, affront some great personage, denounce some cherished institution, behave as badly as possible. When his roommates were invited to the next affair without him, he would feel sorry for himself. To reject while yearning to belong, this was always to be the squaring of the circle for John Reed.

Being a Harvard man remained important in later years. The Harvard Club in New York, Harvard men in Washington and Paris, rooming with Harvard men, continued to matter. It was at a Harvard gathering in Washington that he dramatized his opposition to conscription and America's entrance into the war by refusing to stand up when "The Star-Spangled Banner" was sung. Afterwards it wounded him deeply when they hesitated to speak to him. This concern with Harvard was a part of the lifelong boyishness in Reed, a boyishness noted by all who have written of him, but misinterpreted by those who have set him down as a "playboy."

The Harvard of his day was in a ferment of intellectual radicalism (though that would decline during the war). The Socialist Club, where Reed's classmate Walter Lippmann was holding forth as pundit, got Jack to some of the meetings, but he would not join. His reasons, truth in jest, are suggested in his lines to Lippmann as one

> *Who builds a world, and leaves out all the fun,—*
> *Who dreams a pageant, gorgeous, infinite,*
> *And then leaves all the color out of it,—*
> *Who wants to make the human race, and me,*
> *March to a geometric Q.E.D.*

Reed shopped around, too, at the Single Tax and Anarchist clubs, the Harvard Men's League for Woman's Suffrage, and the other causes enlisting enthusiasm on the campus: modern art, thesis drama, antipuritanism—an apprenticeship for the life he was to find in Greenwich Village.

The one remembered teacher was "Copey," who "stimulated me to find color and strength and beauty in books and in the world, and to express it." Professor Charles Townsend Copeland, in turn, led young Reed back to the tutelage of his father's old friend and comrade in arms, Lincoln Steffens, who was destined to influence him more deeply than any other man for the rest of his days.

Lincoln Steffens was attracted to younger men and greatly enjoyed the influence he could exercise over them. As a topflight journalist, he was always being made an editor of some magazine or daily, yet he hated a desk and four walls and was no editor at all—except for his uncanny ability to think up assignments for himself and his love of scouting for young writers. He had gone to Harvard to ask Copeland for the names of some promising young men. Copey's list included Lippmann, whom Steffens put on the staff of *Everybody's*, and the son of his old friend C. J. Reed, whom he got a job on the *American Magazine*.

Jack's ambitions were modest: "To make a million dol-

lars . . . to get married . . . to write my name in letters of
fire against the sky." When he confided this, "Steffens
looked at me with that lovely smile: 'You can do anything
you want to,' he said . . . There are two men who give me
confidence in myself—Copeland and Steffens . . . More
than any other man, Steff has influenced my mind."

In 1911, Steffens was at the zenith of his reputation—
though the foundations on which it was built were already
eroded. For a few years, America had been much taken
with crusades against Big Business, and against political
corruption. Leading magazines vied with each other to
publish exposés. Wrongly regarded as "the inventor of
muckraking," Steffens was surely its most celebrated prac-
titioner. He contributed a unique off-beat note: liking for
the crooks and grafters, and dislike for the men of his own
class, the reformers to whose crusades his articles contributed.

Publicly Steffens was beginning to affirm that he admired Tammany Boss Richard Croker more than any of
his enemies, and thought J. B. Dill, who had framed the
New Jersey loophole laws for corporations, "one of the
wisest, and, yes, about the rightest man I ever met." He
offered President Charles William Eliot of Harvard a
"course in corruption," not to teach the young how to avoid
it but how to "succeed in their professions," whereupon
President Eliot turned on his heel and walked out of the
room.

Steffens was chagrined when editors would not let
him turn from muckraking to didactic essays to show that
"intelligence was above morality," that there was no science nor certainty to morals, that if you "threw the grafters
out" they were bound to get right back in again. He
wanted to explain that it was "the system" that was corrupt, and the cure quite simple: nationalize all industry,
and industry will *be* government, hence no longer be able
to corrupt it. His valedictory in the field was fittingly en-

titled "An Apology for Graft," its thesis being that "a strong man, however bad, is socially better than a weak man, however good."

Having no patience for the sobering thought that a good fight has to be fought again and again, Steffens' cocksure, arrogant mind cast about for a swift and simple solution. He must work out "the scientific laws of revolution" as previously he had worked out "the scientific laws of corruption." There was a revolution going on in Mexico, but scientists "need more than a single case." Steffens was delighted when revolution broke out in Russia in 1917, and in Italy in 1922. He made a pilgrimage to each. John Reed followed him to Mexico and Russia, but was no longer able to go on the third.

"I would like to spend the evening of my life," Steffens wrote, "watching the morning of a new world." It was a long evening: born twenty-one years before Reed, Steffens died sixteen years after him, pursuing, to the end, his ruling passion, that of influencing and propagandizing young people in favor of revolution.

As he had admired Croker and Dill, so now he admired the strong and ruthless men who were shaping, or misshaping, our age. His admiration for Lenin is too well known to require comment here. No less instructive was his apostrophe to Mussolini:

> It was as if the Author of all things had looked down upon this little planet of His, and seeing the physical, mental, moral confusion said: "I will have a political thunderstorm, big enough for all men to notice and not too big for them to comprehend, and through it I will shoot a blazing thunderbolt that will strike down all their foolish old principles, burn up their dead ideas, and separate the new light I am creating from the darkness men have made." And so he formed Mussolini out of the rib of Italy.

After his "study" of three revolutions, Steffens was sure that "it is useless—it is almost wrong—to fight for the right under our system; petty reforms in politics . . . were impossible, unintelligent, immoral."

He kept urging young people to go to Russia. Personally, he lingered long in a villa in Mussolini's Italy, then settled in "corrupt" Paris and in California's Carmel-by-the-Sea. He "had been to Heaven" (Moscow), but was "so accustomed to Hell" (Paris) that for himself he preferred it. He could "recognize salvation, but could not be saved."

Such was the temper and mind of the distinguished journalist and man of the world who in 1911 took Reed under his care, introducing him to life and art and the men, women, and *isms* of Greenwich Village.

Instantly, Jack fell in love with New York: the Village where he roomed, the theaters, Chinatown, the Fulton Fish Market, the soaring towers, the Hudson smelling of spice and far-off places, the teeming life of the Jewish East Side and Little Italy, Bowery drifters, cheap lodging houses, restaurants "where the foods of the entire world could be found," dope peddlers, streetwalkers, gangsters who killed for hire, Coney Island's garish glitter—all was enchantment. In verses that were derivative but bespoke an eye and a heart all his own, Jack celebrated "the monuments uncouth" of the city's "wild ungovernable youth," the splendors of her achievements and of her still-unfulfilled dreams, the excitements of his own adventures in this splendid and chaotic setting. "In New York I first loved, and first wrote of the things I saw with a fierce joy of creation . . . I was not happy or well long, away from New York . . . I am not now for that matter."[1]

Best of all in the beloved city was his beloved Village. Here were famous men and women, impassioned talk, endless inspiration, unflagging excitement, physical and spiritual adventure. Indeed, when John Reed and three com-

[1] Written in Croton in 1917.

rades from Harvard took rooms in a seedy old building at 42 Washington Square South (and Lincoln Steffens, to be near them, forsook his accustomed luxury to move into rooms on the floor below), Greenwich Village was one of the most exciting spots in the world. The Villagers were creators or devotees of the arts and the *isms*, advocates and exemplars of life lived recklessly, free from the trammels of puritanism, respectability, or convention.

The Village was Freud and Margaret Sanger; Big Bill Haywood, Carlo Tresca, and Emma Goldman; Marx, Henry George, Tolstoy, and Benjamin Tucker; Alfred Stieglitz and Isadora Duncan, and all the other heads of all sorts of movements, some of them with their whole movement in a single head. Editors scouted there. Alongside the established journals new ones sprang up that could not pay a penny, even begged funds from their contributors to keep going. Reed tried to write things that would sell, but as solace for rejection slips found that the Village had an open-hearted, empty-treasuried magazine: the *Masses*. By then, Max Eastman presided over it. Hopeful, vaguely modern, radical, experimental, it was more a Catherine wheel of artists, poets, light and heavy thinkers, and literary pranksters, than a cause or tendency—worlds apart from the *New Masses* and the un-Reed-like "John Reed Clubs" of the thirties. Like the Village itself, it was a home for personal rebels, esthetic rebels, anarchists, socialists, feminists, any *ists* whatsoever. It was perpetually dying for lack of funds, perpetually springing to life again out of the abundance of high spirits that was its real capital.

Before long Jack was, as he had been at Harvard, the managing editor. For one of its resurrections he wrote:

> We refuse to commit ourselves to any course of action, except this: to do with the *Masses* exactly what we please . . . We don't even intend to conciliate our readers . . . Poems, stories, drawings rejected by the capitalistic press on account of their excellence will find a welcome . . . We intend to be arrogant, impertinent,

in bad taste, but not vulgar . . . to attack old systems, old morals, old prejudices . . . to set up new ones in their places . . . We will be bound by no one creed or theory of social reform, but will express them all, providing they be radical . . .

It was a credo for the *Masses* and a personal statement of Jack's own "radicalism." Notable in it was the sense of beleaguered comradeship among these assorted rebels. Though they fought and argued endlessly with each other, they stood shoulder to shoulder against the established. They could write, without mockery, of "the good love of comrades." However much they might disagree with each other's creeds, they defended each other's right to utter and publish what to each might seem good—for none thought then that his heresy might one day become a new orthodoxy, directing inquisition, anathema, and death at all who continued to be rebels. Something of this comradeship in diverse rebellion would sweeten Village life until the thirties, when the blood purges in Moscow would cleave an abyss between those who identified themselves with the driver of the juggernaut and those who felt compassion for its victims.

Moreover, the Village's conception of "the Revolution" was esthetic rather than social. Its high point was the Armory Show of 1913. Mabel Dodge, whose $500 check and busy visits to owners of "advanced" art to get loans of pictures, did much to make the show possible, characterized it well with her usual uninhibited precision:

I felt as though the Exhibition were mine. I really did. It became, over night, my own little Revolution. *I would upset America* . . . It was tragic—I was able to admit that—but the old ways must go, and with them their priests . . . My hand would not shake nor could I allow my personal feelings of pity to halt me. *I was going to dynamite New York* . . .

In 1913, the salon of Mabel Dodge was a unifier of Village life. Like V. F. Calverton in the postwar generation, she had a rare gift for bringing together the atomized particles of our decentralized culture.

Born Mabel Ganson in Buffalo in 1879 (which made her eight years Jack's senior), she would become Mabel Evans in 1900, Mabel Dodge in 1903, marry the painter Maurice Sterne in 1916, and a Hispano-Indian, Antonio Luhan, in 1923. Between the second marriage and the third she came to play a large role in the Village and in John Reed's life.

Returning from three years in her elegant Florentine villa to "ugly, ugly America" and on the way to becoming estranged from her loyal, conventional second husband, she sought to fill the void in her life by turning her beautiful apartment at 23 Fifth Avenue into an open house for everybody that was anybody, and many a nobody. Wealthy, gracious, open-hearted, beautiful, intellectually curious, and quite without a sense of discrimination, she was Bohemia's most successful lion-hunter. "I wanted to know the Heads of things, Heads of movements, Heads of newspapers, Heads of all kinds of groups . . . anything that showed above the tribal pattern." Her hospitality, her capacity for listening, her quiet, encouraging smile, brought together the great, the near-great, and those who came to dream of greatness.

Steffens was one of her lions; he brought the three young Harvard classmates, Lee Simonson, Walter Lippmann, and John Reed. There they could meet of a Wednesday evening the Hapgoods, Jo Davidson, Margaret Sanger, Alexander Berkman, Emma Goldman, Max Eastman, Frances Perkins, Andrew Dasburg, Charles Demuth, Marsden Hartley, Amos Pinchot, Amy Lowell, Edwin Arlington Robinson, Carl Van Vechten, Harry Kemp, Frank Harris, George Sylvester Viereck, John Collier . . . an inexhaustible *Who's Who*.

Sometimes Mrs. Dodge set the subject and selected

the opening speaker; sometimes she shifted the night to make sure that none would know of the gathering except those she personally notified, thus assuring a more uniform group. More often the talk flowed out of the diversity of personalities and convictions. Here, from her *Intimate Memories*, is her account of a "special" evening:

> I switched from the usual Wednesday to a Monday, so that none but more or less radical sympathizers would be there. People who believed that others had the right to kill on principle, if they thought it Right: The Live and Let Live Kind of People.

One evening, they all went to hear Bill Haywood ("a great battered hulk of a man, with one eye gone, and an eminent look in the other") at the home of his mistress, a schoolteacher who lived in the Village. He talked on the desperate Paterson silk strike, police brutality, the silence of the press.

"Why don't you bring the strike to New York and *show* it?" asked Mabel Dodge. "In Madison Square Garden, why not?"

> "I'll do it," cried a voice—and a young man detached himself from the group and assumed a personality before my eyes . . . His olive green eyes glowed softly, his high forehead was like a baby's with light brown curls rolling away from it and two spots of shining light on his temples, making him lovable. His chin was the best . . . the real poet's jawbone . . . eyebrows always lifted . . . generally breathless!

(Max Eastman has affectionately described Jack as having a face "rather like a potato." Curiously, we who knew him found both descriptions, each in its way, correct.)

Reed spent three weeks in Paterson in the midst of the strike, leading the foreign-born workers in revolutionary songs, listening to I.W.W. speakers, getting himself thrown in jail. When the police, who had arrested him "for resisting an officer," found that he was embarrassing them by articles on prison conditions, they threw him out. He headed straight for Mabel Dodge's home. Since it was her idea, he took it for granted that she would work with him on it. His exuberance dragged her into an enterprise alien and indifferent to her nature. Thus was born "The Pageant of the Paterson Strike."

His scenario was rather bare and simple. But the novelty of masses of strikers and I.W.W. leaders as actors gave the performance an unexpected intensity. Jack appeared in his own pageant to lead the strikers in revolutionary songs.

It is hard work to fill Madison Square Garden. The dollar and two-dollar seats remained almost empty until workers and strikers were let in free or at ten cents a seat. Instead of making money, the pageant ended with a deficit. The long strike was finally lost. But Jack did not stay to learn the results. The day after the pageant, he and Mabel left for Europe.

When he came to the Village he had a girl he wanted to marry. For the first five months, he wrote, "I was sentimental about it and remained chaste." Then she was forgotten, and he followed a roving eye and fancy into a succession of affairs, all "wonderful" but none deep. When he told his current love, "Rose, I don't love you; I love Mable Dodge," she shed a few tears on his shoulder and sobbed, "I am so unhappy," then suddenly raised her eyes in surprise and said: "Why, no I'm not!"

But his love for Mabel Dodge was different. It must have been a possessive, even oppressive passion. She owns herself to have been jealous of the stones of Venice, of the way he felt about history, and the way he said, "The things *Men* have done!" ("Past or present, I did not care what they had done . . . I jumped into the automobile and returned to Florence, leaving him there to it.") She was jealous of the Harvard friends who soon came to take him

on stag explorations. She was jealous of Mexico and his
life with Villa's band, when Steffens had him sent there as
a correspondent; jealous of the Great War when he became
a correspondent in Europe.

> Good-bye, my darling [he wrote in one such quarrel]
> —You smother me. You crush me. You want to kill my
> spirit. I love you better than life but do not want to
> die in my spirit. I am going away to save myself. For-
> give me. I love you. I love you. Reed.

Yet he returned, and the torment continued. Suddenly, after a year and some months, love for Reed died
in her as swiftly as it had flared up. Yet he continued to
count on it, had editors send her reports on him, wrote her
of brief affairs with other girls and his enduring love for
her.

For her part, she could not see why they "should not
continue to be close friends." She tried to house him as her
guest in the attic of the farmhouse she took with Maurice
Sterne, but he could not act out this desperate Village
convention. "Why can't people *live* their theories, any-
way?" she cried. Not until December, 1915, was Jack able
to break the spell. Then he wrote:

> I think I've found Her at last. She's wild, brave and
> straight—and graceful and lovely to look at. In this
> spiritual vacuum, this unfertilized soil [he was writing
> from Portland where he was visiting his mother], she
> has grown (how, I can't imagine) into an artist. She
> is coming to New York to get a job—with me, I hope.
> I think she's the first person I ever loved without
> reservation.

The new love was Louise Bryant Trullinger, wife of a
Portland dentist, unhappy with Portland and with her husband, hungering for New York and adventure. New York
took on new radiance as Reed showed her its wonders.
Thus began a stormy love, broken by intermittent affairs
on both sides, yet continuing. In November, 1916, when

Jack went to the hospital to get his ailing kidney removed, they were married. In 1917, and again in 1919, she went to Russia when Reed was there, the first time as a correspondent in her own right. She was with him in Moscow when he died.

Following Reed's loves we have run ahead of his life as a writer. In November, 1913, he went to Mexico to report for the *Metropolitan* and the *World*. To Reed the Mexican Revolution was a pageant, a succession of adventures, a delight to the eye, a chance to discover that he was not afraid of bullets. His reports overflow with life and movement: simple, savage men, capricious cruelty, warm comradeship, splashes of color, bits of song, fragments of social and political dreams, personal peril, gay humor, reckless daring. Neither Steffens, who joined and counted on Venustiano Carranza, nor Reed, who celebrated the pastoral dreams and bold deeds of Pancho Villa, had any real notion of the Mexican maze. But Reed's mingling of personal adventure with camera-eye close-ups lighted by a poet's vision made superb reporting. The book he made of them, *Insurgent Mexico*, despite its careless ignorance of men, events, and forces, and even of Spanish, which he mangled in the ballads he quoted, was closer to the feeling of Mexico in revolution than most things that Americans have written on it. When he returned to New York, he found that he had a reputation as a war correspondent.

When war broke out in Europe in 1914, he was asked to cover it for the *Metropolitan*. First Italy—nothing worth reporting. France, having settled down to trench warfare, seemed dull and gloomy to him, with none of the excitement of Pancho Villa's hard-riding bands. He tried England—no exciting story there either.

"The real war," he wrote, echoing Steffens, "is a clash of traders." Like most Village radicals, he was inclined to sympathize with Germany as the "underdog," the latecomer among the trading and colonial nations who had arrived when everything was pre-empted. Not much to choose between the sides, but the Entente seemed "more hypocritical." His most violent language was reserved for England, who

> grips the Red Sea, sucks the blood from all India, menaces a half billion human beings from Hong Kong, owns all Australia, half North America, and half of Africa . . . the great intriguer, sitting like a spider in the web of nations . . . It was England's will that Germany should be destroyed.

The *Metropolitan* did not print his article.

Taking advantage of the fact that America was neutral, he left for Germany and its front in occupied France. His accounts are in general favorable to the occupiers. He spent a night under fire in the foremost trench, where he could see the French lines and the dead in no man's land. After a night in rain and mud, under a hail of shrapnel and shells, he was asked by a German lieutenant whether he would like to have a shot. With a rifle borrowed from a German soldier, he fired two shots at daybreak in the general direction of the French. This escapade, reported by a fellow correspondent, was to cause trouble for him later in tsarist Russia, be held against him in Washington, cause him to be barred from France. That is how John Reed came to be transferred to the eastern front, with Boardman Robinson as his artist-illustrator. The results of their collaboration appeared in 1916 as *The War in Eastern Europe*.

His tour of duty as a European war correspondent was a disappointment to editors, friends, and to Jack himself. His daring recklessness, his poet's vision and camera-eye, his shallow explanations of the "traders' war," were not enough to work with in the grim, vast, irreducible stalemate. "I have come to hate Europe," he wrote his mother.

The eastern front proved scarcely more rewarding. Having worked his way up through the Balkans into

Russia without permission from the Russian authorities and pursued by the story of his two shots at the French, he landed in a Russian jail. It was sixteen days before American officials could arrange his peaceful and ignominious departure. With his usual boyish exuberance, he had written on his passport for the benefit of the Russian authorities: "I am a German and an Austrian spy. I do it for money. Reed."

Despite misadventure, his brief stay in Russia had made him a Russophile:

> Russian ideals are the most exhilarating, Russian thought the freest, Russian art the most exuberant; Russian food and drink are to me the best, and Russians themselves are, perhaps, the most interesting human beings that exist . . . There the people live as if they knew it were a great empire . . . Every one acts just as he feels like acting, and says just what he wants to. There are no particular times for getting up or going to bed or eating dinner, and there is no conventional way of murdering a man, or making love.

It was tsarist Russia of late 1915 that he was celebrating.

Back in America in 1916, Reed was alarmed by his country's drift toward war. With Henrietta Rodman, Franklin Giddings, Carlton Hayes, John Dewey, he signed an appeal to Socialists to vote for Wilson because "he kept us out of war." George Creel organized a group of writers to re-elect Wilson; among them were Steffens, Howe, Zona Gale, Hutch Hapgood, George Cram Cook, Susan Glaspell, and Reed. America's swift entrance into the war on the side of the Allies, even before Wilson had pronounced his second inaugural, goes far to explain the subsequent fury of Village radicalism.

After the removal of his long-ailing kidney, the publication of a slender and undistinguished volume of poems, the writing of the essay on the first twenty-nine years of life, and exemption from the draft because of the kidney operation, Jack sought an assignment to Russia where the Tsar had fallen and a revolution begun. In his "Almost Thirty," Jack wrote:

> I must find myself again. Some men seem to get their direction early . . . I have no idea what I shall be or do one month from now. Whenever I have tried to become some one thing, I have failed; . . . only by drifting with the wind I have found myself. . . . I wish with all my heart that the proletariat would rise and take their rights . . . But I am not sure any more that the working class is capable of revolution, peaceful or otherwise. The War has been a terrible shatterer of faith . . . And yet, I cannot give up the idea that out of democracy will be born the new world—richer, braver, freer, more beautiful . . . I don't know what I can do to help . . . My happiness is built on the misery of other people . . . that fact poisons me, disturbs my serenity, makes me write propaganda when I would rather play.

It was in this mood that John Reed, on August 17, 1917, set sail with Louise Bryant for Russia.

He arrived late that August with an exalted preconception of what he was going to see. His own civilization was in crisis; his country had gone to war. He was ready to support the party that wanted to take Russia out of the war and, he hoped, put an end to war. It was a simple, comforting, and by no means ignoble belief.

Of Lenin's authoritarian party structure and organization creed he knew nothing: so much the freer was his fancy to endow the conflict and chaos he was to witness with the form and substance of his own dream.

To Boardman Robinson he wrote: "We are in the middle of things and believe me it's thrilling. For color and terror and grandeur this makes Mexico look pale."

His Russian was even sketchier than his Spanish, but

no matter. For worker and peasant there was a gay smile and the sputtering of *Ya amerikanskii sotsialist!* And, since all Russia was talking and yearning to unburden its soul, any number of officers, intellectuals, and political leaders could talk to him in English, French, or German. Makers of history and those being unmade by it, veteran fighters for freedom smarting under the new-found epithet, "counter-revolutionist"—who would refuse to talk to an American reporter who was so ardent, attractive, and boyish a listener? In the back of every meeting into which Jack shouldered his way, there was always someone to answer his perpetual, breathless "Say, what's going on here?"

He made his way into the Smolny, where the Bolsheviks had their headquarters; into the City Duma, stronghold of liberal democracy; into the soviets of workers and soldiers and into the soviets of peasants; into barracks, factory meetings, street processions, halls, courts; into the Constituent Assembly, which the Bolsheviks dispersed; into the Winter Palace when it was being defended by student officers and a woman's battalion, and again when it was being overrun and looted. All Russia was meeting, and John Reed was meeting with it.

If two shots from a German Mauser did not make him cease to be a neutral in the Great War, in this "class war pure and simple" he strove to be a participant. Twice he addressed crowds in the Cirque Moderne, bringing fraternal greetings (from whom?), being presented as spokesman for the American Socialist party (which he was not), and as a man under indictment in far-off America (which, as an editor of the antiwar *Masses*, he was). He addressed Bolshevik factory meetings, careened around the city on one of their trucks hurling out leaflets he could not read, joined the looting of the Winter Palace, carrying off some notes of a doomed minister and a jewel-handled sword concealed under his coat.

With his poet's blood and rebel's heart he decided what to believe. Then, with the artist's gift for selection, heightening and unifying, he assimilated all the chaotic impressions into a picture more impressive and more beautiful than life itself.

When Boardman Robinson reproached him once with "But it didn't happen that way!" his answer was an *ad hominem* of artist to artist. "What the hell difference does it make?" And, seizing one of Robinson's sketches: "She didn't have a bundle as big as that . . . he didn't have so full a beard." Drawing, Robinson explained, was not a matter of photographic accuracy but of over-all impression. "Exactly," Reed cried in triumph, "that is just what I am trying to do!"

Yet there is nothing of the mean, deliberate lie about John Reed's *Ten Days That Shook the World.* A good reporter, always in the thick of things, he possessed an honest sense of vivid detail that makes one page refute another.

He idealized the masses. He believed the ridiculous legend, born perhaps of his own dream, that the Bolshevik Central Committee, after having rejected the idea of an insurrection, was made to reverse itself by a single speech of a rank and file workingman. (There was such a reversal, but the "rank and file workingman" was Lenin!) Though literacy was declining all through the war, and would continue to decline for years after, Reed wrote sincerely: "All Russia was learning to read." A few pages later, without any sense of contradiction, comes this vivid scene:

> We did not notice a change in the attitude of the soldiers and Red guards around us . . . A small group followed us until by the time we reached the great picture gallery . . . about a hundred men surged in after us. One giant of a soldier stood in our path, his face dark with sullen suspicion. "Who are you?" he growled. The others massed slowly around, staring and beginning to mutter . . . I produced our passes from

the Military Revolutionary Committee. The soldier took them gingerly, turned them upside down and looked at them without comprehension. Evidently he could not read. "Bumagi!" ("Papers!") said he with contempt. The mass slowly began to close in, like wild catttle around a cow-puncher on foot . . .

It was an officer, from the intelligentsia Reed professed to despise, who—frightened and sweating—managed to save Jack and Louise from instant lynching. Twice he is nearly lynched and saved by an officer, but Reed never permits himself to doubt that lynchings are salutary and the mob just.

For Reed the Revolution is holy. As a devout Christian may believe that on the night of the Savior's birth "no spirit dares stir abroad; the nights are wholesome, then no planets strike, no fairy takes, nor witch hath power to charm, so hallow'd and so gracious is the time"—so Reed writes of the night Lenin seized power: "On that night not a single hold-up occurred, not a single robbery." The same impression of sacredness is repeated three days later: "Quiet the city lay, not a hold-up, not a robbery, not even a drunken fight."

Yet this does not prevent his quoting Trotsky on the all-embracing wave of drunkenness that accompanied the seizure of power. Nor prevent his reproducing an order showing that the drunken wave continued into late December. It is instructive to compare Reed's "Quiet the city lay" with the plaint of Antonov-Ovseenko, leader of the attack on the Winter Palace:

> The Preobrazhensky regiment got completely drunk while guarding the wine cellars of the Palace . . . The Pavlovsky regiment did not withstand temptation either . . . Mixed, picked guards were sent; they, too, got drunk. Members of the regimental committees were assigned . . . These succumbed too. Men of the armored brigades were ordered to disperse the crowds—they paraded to and fro, then began to sway suspiciously

. . . An attempt was made to flood the cellars. The fire
brigades got drunk . . . The whole city was infected
with this drinking madness . . .

How could Reed not have seen it?

Though his "vision" raced ahead of his eyes, creating
its own illusion, yet his eyes were everywhere. And his
person, too. He tried to see it all and put it all on paper.
The dream of the Bolsheviks, the realities of their deeds,
and the tension between the dream and the reality are in
his pages. If he did not comprehend the meaning of the
large events, what observer or participant did? He understood less and misunderstood more than many, so that
one of the personages of whom he wrote would say to
me of his book: "The work of an innocent who did not
know whether he was attending a wedding or a funeral!"
It was a funeral—of Russia's newly won liberties, achieved
after a century of struggle. If Jack thought that he was
witnessing the wedding of liberty and justice destined to
live together happily ever after, so well does he report
that we can see the acts of burial even as he sings of
nuptials.

As a repository of facts for the historian, his book is
bursting with precious material: interviews, speeches, resolutions, press clippings. One of his habits was to tear down
a specimen of every poster or proclamation for future
translation. The book is full of quotations from these
documents, and illustrated by photos of many of them—
a priceless opportunity for the historian to enter into a
time that has passed.

Whether because of or despite the dream that possessed him, as literature Reed's book is the finest piece
of eye-witness reporting the Revolution produced. It is
his true monument, more enduring than the name carved on
the Kremlin wall.

After the *Ten Days*, the rest of his life is anticlimax.
He tried to become a communist politician, but as a

politician he was out of his element. After his return to
the United States in the spring of 1918, he sat on tire-
some committees and toured the country speaking on
the Russian Revolution. Despairing of politics, he sought
martyrdom. Though the country was in the grip of wartime fever and hysteria, officials returned the posters they
had seized from him on his landing; the indictments against
him as an editor of the *Masses,* as opponent of the war,
as "inciter to riot," as preacher of sedition and revolution,
all were quashed, or dismissed, or ended in acquittal. He
helped to split the Socialist party, got caught up in a
frustrating split in the nascent Communist Party, and all
the while longed to get back to the old life of adventure
and poetry. Twice he fled from cheerless meetings to seek
out Sherwood Anderson. "If I were dead sure I had something on the ball as a poet . . ." he told Anderson wistfully.

He wrote propaganda articles on America, the world
situation, communism. They are dull, foolish, barely readable.

Then came the chance to return to adventure. The
occasion was petty: to present the case of one of the
splinters of the new communist movement against the
other, before the Communist International.

It was a perilous quest to get to the Red Mecca. Fear-
ful of the contagion of revolution, the West had set up
a *cordon sanitaire* around Russia, as later the Kremlin
would set up its own "iron curtain" against the contagion
of freedom. Denied a passport, Jack sailed with forged
identification papers as Jim Gormley, stoker on a Scandinavian vessel, in September of 1919. Though his health
had been weakened by his kidney operation and his ir-
regular habits, "Gormley" did his work satisfactorily as a
stoker—until he jumped ship in Norway. From there he
stowed away in a greasy pile of rags on a ship bound for
Finland and was smuggled across the Finnish frontier
into Russia.

It was not the Russia of his dreams. He was hurt by

the spectacle of hunger, misery, breakdown, apathy, above all by the way the new bureaucracy was beginning to lavish care on itself in the midst of universal misery. As in 1917, he insisted on living like the unprivileged. He sought to preserve the fragments of his dream by attributing everything to the civil war and the blockade and ignoring the contribution made by Lenin's absurd outlawing of trade between town and country and nationalization of everything "down to the last inkwell."

"From every trip," wrote Angelica Balabanoff, then Secretary of the Communist International, "he would come back to the capital less and less cheerful, more and more sad and preoccupied . . . because of the superfluous sufferings of the people, those which could have been avoided."

Reed made two attempts to return to America. On the second he was caught in Finland, and after more than two months of hunger and filth in a Finnish jail, was deported back to Moscow. He had scurvy; his arms and legs were swollen from malnutrition. But he continued to insist on living like the masses.

Now he decided to wait for the Second Congress of the Communist International in Moscow. From it came another sort of disillusion to which his heart was peculiarly vulnerable.

The order of business for the Second Congress had been determined by Lenin. Having concluded that the great push for world revolution had failed, and with it the attempt to smash the old socialist parties and trade unions, Lenin set it as the task of all revolutionaries to return to or infiltrate the old trade unions. As always, Lenin took it for granted that whatever conclusion he had come to in evaluation and in strategy and tactics was infallibly right. In the Comintern, as in his own party, his word was law.

But the British delegates had worked out their own attitude toward the Labor Party, and the American delegates were hostile to the American Federation of Labor and supported the I.W.W. As for Reed, he had been brought to the labor movement by the I.W.W.'s strike in Paterson. The I.W.W. leaders had gone to jail en masse for opposing the war, while the A.F. of L. had been pro-war and supported "the system." The A.F. of L. must be smashed, the I.W.W. supported.

That Lenin had made up his mind for America did not impress him. It was the Americans who knew their land and had to determine the policies they were to carry out in it. Jack prepared for a fight. On behalf of thirty delegates from the English-speaking countries, he introduced two motions: to put the trade-union question at the top of the order of business, and to add English to the already adopted German, French, and Russian, as an official language of debate. With Zinoviev in the chair, the motions were not so much voted down as simply ruled out.

> As I was the only translator [writes Angelica Bala-banoff] I remember the protest of the English-speaking delegations because the Chair decided not to have the speeches translated into English. I was naïve enough to believe that this "omission" was to save time or transla-tion work. When I said I would gladly translate into English, too, my offer was not taken into consideration.

Thus Reed could neither have his arguments seriously presented to other delegations nor find out what was being said against him. He had seen steam-rollers before, but never one like this.

Shunted to the Trade Union Commission, he was told that the matter had been "settled" and he must obey discipline. Radek accused him of sabotage. Mocking him for believing that America could be taken from the Rocke-fellers and Morgans, but not the A.F. of L. from the Gom-perses, Zinoviev mobilized obedient henchmen, lined up delegations on the basis of loyalty to the Russians, held meetings without notifying Reed of time or place.

Reed would not give in. A rebel, not a robot, he was not made to be a cog in a ruthless machine. The Comintern, even then, was on its way to becoming a "monolith," appropriate symbol not of the diversity of rebellious humanity, but of the solid block of granite that might serve as a tombstone over men's hope of freedom. Not one of the impatient and ardent rebels who had flocked from all over the world to Moscow would long endure in the Comintern. Even Angelica Balabanoff, despite her two decades of activity in the socialist parties of two nations and the Second and Third Internationals, would last only a few months longer.

By the time the Congress was over, Angelica was the only Russian leader to whom Jack could still talk and confide his doubts and sorrows. Yet he still had fight in him, and wrote an article for his party's journal in which he said: "Nobody in Russia seems to understand industrial unionism . . . At the next Congress these theses must be altered."

But for him there was to be no "next Congress."

"When he came to see me after the Congress," Dr. Balabanoff wrote, "he was in a terrible state of depression. He looked old and exhausted. The experience had been a terrible blow."

Either during the Congress or right after it, Reed resigned his post as member of the Executive Committee of the International, as a protest—his communist biographers have circumspectly said—"on an organizational question." Somehow he was made to withdraw his resignation, and somehow, despite broken health and spirit, made to go with Zinoviev, Radek, and a trainload of delegates to a Congress of the "Toiling Peoples of the East" in Baku. The hues and costumes of the men from the East, and their sudden way of drawing and raising aloft curved scimitars to approve a resolution, stirred Jack's romantic heart. But the demagogy of Zinoviev and Radek, and the luxury on the special train running through a land of famine, sickened him.

Back in Moscow, Jack took to his bed with typhus. How much the virus, how much the ravaged body, how much the broken spirit prevailed, we can only guess. To Angelica Balabanoff, and to Louise Bryant, who had just managed to come to Moscow from America, it seemed, as Angelica was to write, that "the moral and nervous shock had deprived him of the wish to live, of that love of life that was so prominent in his character."

When Kobetsky, technical secretary of the International, wrote to Lenin that Reed was dead, Lenin answered:

> Comrade Kobetsky!
> 1. Your report (that is the report of the physician you sent me) and the note, should be sent abroad.
> 2. Who is in charge of the Hotel Lux? Its remodelling for the Comintern? The management part?
>
> Lenin 18/X

With Reed's death, rebellion ended. As the author of what Lenin rightly esteemed to be the best book on his seizure of power, Reed was given a state funeral. Feeling that she could not speak of him without speaking of his last days, Angelica Balabanoff refused to deliver an address or even attend his funeral. "I knew Reed would have understood . . . Most of the people who commemorated him were not entitled to do so. Their speeches *had* to be cold, official, conventional."

A decade passed, and the ashes lay forgotten, along with the sturdy example of independence. Then Stalin began to utilize the names of the safely dead, and to purge the living, including most of the men who figured so prominently in Reed's book: Trotsky, Antonov-Ovseenko, Bukharin, Radek, Zinoviev, Kamenev, and so many more. *Ten Days That Shook the World* was alive with their names and deeds, so it too was suppressed, first in Russia and then wherever the Comintern owned the copyright through a manipulated publisher, as in England.

But in America, John Reed's name was exploited through the John Reed Clubs. A biography was invented for him in which rebelliousness and manly opposition to dictatorial authority found no place.

Then suddenly, the "line" changed. In the new "Popular Front" period of the nineteen-thirties, revolution had to be played down. Jack's name was too inseparable from the idea of the October Revolution. It was dropped as remorselessly as it had been previously used; overnight, the John Reed Club became the League of American Writers.

With Stalin's death, the wheel of fortune took another turn. Reed's book reappeared in Russia; Lenin's cold letter to Kobetsky was published as evidence of Lenin's "concern for American writers."

Still John Reed's spirit evades official control and goes its own characteristic way. It lives on in the record of his rebellious, adventurous, generously romantic, perpetually immature, brave poet's life, in his colorful *Insurgent Mexico,* and, at its enduring best, in *Ten Days That Shook the World.*

2

The
Catholic
Communist

BIG JIM LARKIN appeared in our midst surrounded by legend. The year was 1917; I for one had not known him earlier. Though many of the legends surrounding him could not have been so, they seemed appropriate to his person, and on the whole believable.

James Robert Larkin was a big-boned, large-framed man, broad shoulders held not too high nor too proudly, giving him an air of stooping over ordinary men when he was speaking to them. Bright blue eyes flashed from dark heavy brows; a long fleshy nose, hollowed out cheeks, prominent cheek bones, a long, thick neck, the cords of which stood out when he was angry, a powerful, stubborn chin, a head longer and a forehead higher than in most men, suggesting plenty of room for the brain pan. Big Jim was well over six feet tall, so that I, a six-footer, felt small when I looked up into his eyes. Long arms and legs, great hands like shovels, big, rounded shoes, shaped in front like the rear of a canal boat, completed the picture.

The legend surrounding him with the greatest glory was that he had personally participated in the armed defense of Liberty Hall, Dublin, during the Easter, 1916, uprising, and, when all was lost, had escaped from the rear of the Hall disguised as an old crone. The legend was utterly incompatible with those huge hands and feet, that long, powerful, masculine face, those great shoulders. Stoop as he would, he could not have passed off as an old crone. But I was inclined to believe it until, years later, I learned that he had left Dublin for America in 1914 to get guns and money from the Germans, and could not possibly have been in Liberty Hall on Easter Sunday, 1916, since he did not return to Ireland until he was released from a New York State jail in 1923.

When Larkin spoke, his blue eyes flashed and sparked. He roared and thundered, sputtered and—unless a stage separated him from the public—sprayed his audience with spittle. Sometimes an unruly forelock came down on his forehead as he moved his head in vigorous emphasis. Impulsive, fiery, passionate, swift at repartee, highly personal, provocative, and hot tempered in attack, strong and picturesque of speech, Larkin's language was rich in the turns of Irish poetic imagery sprinkled with neologisms of his own devising. Particularly in front of an Irish or an Irish-American audience, or an audience of bewildered foreign-born socialists unprepared for poetry and religion in Marxist oratory, he was the most powerful speaker in the left wing socialist movement.

Born in the slums of Liverpool in 1876, he was twenty years my senior. In 1917, when I became aware of his presence in America, he had just turned forty-one. His grandfather, an Irish Fenian who had fled to Liverpool, had communicated to him the picturesque flavor and poetic richness of speech and accent—and a keen sense of Ireland's wrongs. Orphaned when in the fourth grade in school, Jim thenceforth had to shift for himself, working at a multitude of trades and occupations: delivery boy for a butcher, painter and paperhanger (for which his tall frame with its built-in stepladder fitted him admirably),

factory worker, dairy worker, sailor both in merchant ves-
sels and in the American navy, ship's fireman, mechanical
engineer, docker, soldier, an organizer of the Irish Republican Army, labor leader, pamphleteer, journalist, editor, and, while in prison in the United States, baker, textile
worker, tinsmith, and bookbinder. In addition to these
varied pursuits, he had been a professional soccer player,
a social worker, always an agitator, and, to the end of his
days, a temperance advocate who would not touch strong
drink.

More remarkable than his many professions was his
compound of beliefs. An Irish Nationalist to the core of
his being, he was at the same time a revolutionary socialist
and internationalist. One of the founders of the left wing
of the Socialist Party and a brilliant communist orator in
the formative days of the American Communist Party, he
was nevertheless, as befits an Irishman, a devout Catholic,
a true son of his Church, believing in its dogmas, its creed,
the authority of its hierarchical powers, and every detail
of its rule.

In America, he was anti-war not because he opposed
war for the freedom of Ireland, but because he opposed
America's entrance into the war on the side of England.
Yet he was not anti-English either, not anti-Protestant. He
was not pro-German, though he accepted German money
to buy arms for The Irish Rebellion, and, no doubt, did
things to block England's war efforts. Surrounded as he
was by Irish seamen, Irish longshoremen, Irish couriers,
he had no difficulty arranging for a clandestine trip over-
seas, nor getting commands carried out by an army of
followers.

Yet the Connolly Club, which he founded on West
29th Street in New York City by the simple expedient of
leading a band of his followers in capturing for the left
wing of the Socialist Party the old Socialist Party's headquarters by breaking the lock, and then moving in bodily,
with his cookstove for frying eggs and Irish bacon, his

Irish Worker, his mimeograph machine, and his hangers on had room for workingmen of all nationalities, Jewish cloakmakers, Scotsmen and Englishmen, Germans, Bulgarians, Yugo-Slavs, Russians, Greenwich Villagers. Wide-eyed they listened to the poetry of Larkin's speech, his intemperate polemics, his crotchets, his mixture of creeds.

To his home in Patchin Place, where he likewise held forth, there came men of all nations, Irish labor leaders, American leaders of Irish descent, representatives of the German Embassy and German agents, American left wing socialists, Greenwich Village Pacifists, members of the I.W.W. His lieutenants included a Canadian Irishman named Curley, Tom O'Flaherty, Patrick Quinlan of the I.W.W., Shaemus O'Shael, Eadmonn MacAlpine. It was through his rebel network of seamen and longshoremen in New York Harbor that he fixed up the trip that took John Reed to Soviet Russia with forged seaman's papers, wearing a fisherman's shirt and passing as a sailor on some Scandinavian ship.

When Larkin voiced his religious opinions, it was with no reticence, defiantly, as something he had a right to believe in. It might seem strange to his atheistic auditors, schooled in agnosticism, or dogmatic materialism of one kind or another, but for him Catholicism was the unifying creed of Irishmen, the banner of their struggle for freedom, the foundation of his simple socialism. Once at a meeting in the New Star Casino he shocked his audience by flaunting the cross that he always wore buttoned in his shirt. As its gold glinted, he cried to his audience: "There is no antagonism between the Cross and socialism! A man can pray to Jesus the Carpenter, and be a better socialist for it. Rightly understood, there is no conflict between the vision of Marx and the vision of Christ. I stand by the Cross and I stand by Karl Marx. Both *Capital* and the *Bible* are to me Holy Books."

Marx would have been as surprised and shocked as Larkin's self-righteous audience, and so indeed would many a Christian Father. But that was Larkin's socialism, behind it was a long tradition of Christian socialism, in England, in America, and in the streets of Dublin. The American socialists of the moment had forgotten yesterday's socialism with the Reverend Bouck White's *The Call of the Carpenter,* as they had the Christian socialism of Great Britain. Though the conservative wing was then dominant in the Catholic Church, there was even at that moment in Washington, a Catholic clerical group headed by Father John A. Ryan, who was concerned with labor organization and the welfare of the workingmen, in a spirit not out of line with the somewhat eclectic socialism of Jim Larkin.

Pope Gregory XVI had voiced the Church's awareness of the new problems of the working class in urban, industrialized society a decade before the *Communist Manifesto* was written. Many churchmen urged upon wealthy parishioners the use of Christian principles in dealing with workingmen and their families. Pope Leo's *Rerum Novarum* (*Of Modern Matters*—otherwise known as the "Encyclical on The Condition of Labor") recognized the Church's responsibility for a society generous and just to the poor and to the laborer, and urged that many of the tenets of socialism, freed from class hatred and atheism, and no doubt from the turbulent belligerence of Jim Larkin, were entirely consistent with Christian doctrine.

While America was at war, the National Catholic Council (today known as the National Catholic Welfare Council), whose leading figure then was Father John A. Ryan, came out in favor of the organization of the unskilled workingmen, at the same time criticizing the American Federation of Labor for its too exclusive concentration on the skilled crafts. It urged more attention to the migratory, the foreign born, the working men in mass production industries and what social workers call "the underprivileged." What was this but the new unionism or the "one big unionism" of Connolly and Larkin? The state-

ment of the Council was signed by Bishops Muldoon,
Rockford, Schrembs, Hayes, Russell, and, of course, Father
Ryan. It opposed state ownership of industry and "complete
socialism" but favored consumers' cooperatives, and, where
possible, producers' cooperatives in which the workingmen
should own their own means of production, and also urged
a steadily larger participation of labor in the ownership
and management of industry. "The full possibilities of in-
creased production," the Council held, "will not be realized
so long as the majority of the workers remain mere wage
earners." They must "become owners, at least in part, of
the instruments of production." It is to be noted, their
manifesto concluded, "that this particular modification of
the existing order, however far-reaching and though in-
volving to a great extent the abolition of the wage system,
would not mean the abolition of private ownership. The
instruments of production would still be owned by individuals, not by the State." This was not very different from
Larkin's conceptions of socialism, and in America more
than in Ireland, justified his faith in the "more Christian
members" in the hierarchy.

In Ireland no unionism would have been possible
against the beliefs of the Church. But among the men
and women facing Jim Larkin in the New Star Casino,
Larkin's was a strange, incredible voice and creed. Whether
angered at their reception of his views, or enjoying the
sensation he was creating, or driven by an inner compulsion to express his beliefs, Larkin continued to hold the
golden cross before him on its chain and proclaim, "I belong to the Catholic Church. I stand by the Cross and the
Bible and I stand by Marx and his *Manifesto*. I believe
in the creed of the Church, apostolic, Catholic, and Roman. I believe in its saints and its martyrs, their struggles
and the sufferings of my people. The history of Ireland is
full of the same spirit, the same struggles, the same sufferings, the struggles and sufferings of my people. In my land
this is not held against a socialist. It speaks for him. I defy

any man here or anywhere to challenge my standing as a Catholic, as a socialist, or as a revolutionist. We of the Irish Citizen's Army take communion before we ge into battle. We confess our sins. We seek absolution. If a bullet strikes, we hope to have the last rites administered to us before our souls leave our bodies. We do not let the Church stand in the way of our struggle, but neither do we let our struggle stand in the way of the Church."

Larkin's natural rebelliousness was intensified when at eighteen he shipped for America as a stowaway, was caught and put in irons on shipboard, then jailed for a month in New York. America did not yet have the system of deportation of immigrants which was to come as a by-product of the period between the wars. In jail he read American writers as earlier he had read Irish and English writers. Combative by nature, he was reflective, too, and a romantic who always saw himself as the spokesman and leader of some gallant fight.

There was much in Irish history to nourish that romantic streak in him, for Ireland's struggles were a succession of glorious lost causes centering around men like Wolfe Tone and Robert Emmet, whose lives and martyrdoms were to him the history of his beloved land and a scenario for his own life. "Let us rejoice," he wrote of Robert Emmet, "that it was vouchsafed to this nation that such a man was given to us . . . the city beautiful that was so plain and dear to him shall also be the city beautiful for us." And on Wolfe Tone (Larkin was somehow a little warmer and friendler to me than to most Americans because I shared one of Wolfe Tone's two names) he wrote, "It was that love, that intense desire to serve Ireland, that was the reason for the man. . . . Tone was a Republican, a nationalist, an internationalist, a man who sought liberty not for himself but for his fellows—liberty of thought, liberty of action, liberty to live—liberty has reason to be proud of her son Tone."

In his pictures of Tone and Emmet appeared the traits
that he liked to believe he possessed himself. It was of
himself and his own aspirations as much as of Robert
Emmet that he was speaking when he wrote in the *Irish
Worker* of March 8, 1913, "Whenever or wherever a rebel
is born, breaks a chain, or glorifies her cause by his death,
all lovers and worshippers of liberty rejoice at the birth,
the tug at the chain, or mourn the loss of the valiant comrade, irrespective of what family or nation the particular
rebel belongs to. The fight for liberty is not a parochial
or national affair. It is a universal struggle, and all nations,
all free men and women rejoice when the devotee of liberty shatters another link of ignorance or slavery. The very
sound of the word *Freedom*, let it be to many or to your-
self, you will enjoy a thrill that few enjoy, but what a
satisfaction and awakening to the soul it must be to have
struck one blow for the cause. . . ." The style is the style
of Larkin's oratory as well as of his writing. The slight
incoherence of structure, the flaming intensity of feeling,
the ardent love of liberty were common to both his oral
and his written speech.

This internationalist spoke of patriotism "as the most
beautiful thing on earth, aye in Heaven." When he saw
northern and southern Irishmen at war with each other
and refusing to cooperate for common aims, he admonished
them, "Be men! Be Irishmen, and don't disgrace your-
selves." He was angered by the partition of Ireland, but
would not admit that the dividing line should separate
Irish workingmen North and South, or set workers in Belfast at odds with workers in Dublin. He emphasized what
united them, not what divided them. To show what it
meant to be "a man and an Irishman and not disgrace your-
self," he marched arm in arm with Protestant Orangemen
of the North saying as he did so, "Protestants can follow
the banners of William of Orange and Catholics can, too,
for they are the colors which the Pope blessed." In the
Irish Worker he wrote to the men of the North, "Workers

of Belfast, stop your damned nonsense. . . . Let not what
masquerades as religion in this country divide you. . . .
Not as Catholics or Protestants, as Nationalists or Unionists, but as Belfast men and workers stand together and
don't be misled by the employers' game of dividing the
Catholic and the Protestant." He was as Catholic as any
other true southern Irishman, but the Church was not
to be permitted to stand as a barrier between men with
common needs and common hopes. That might pass as religion for some, but not for him.

Despite all his trades and professions, Jim Larkin was
first and foremost a workingman. When he became a foreman of a group of dockworkers in Liverpool, he sought to
organize them and to reform their habits. He neither drank
nor smoked himself, engaging in a one man crusade against
the drunkenness which was taken for granted among the
rough, poor dockworkers over whom he acquired influence. No one ever heard foul language from his lips. He
could be as hot tempered as any man, indeed, hotter, but
the temper expressed itself in withering repartee, angry
condemnation, and scorn, sputtering, unforgettable epithets, never in obscenity.

He absorbed his socialism and his laborism from the
slums and the docks, his Irish nationalism from his family
and fellow workingmen of Irish origin. Like these he had
a taste for combat and loudmouthed controversy that lifted
his voice above the voice of others and made rough men
look up to him. Along with socialism came what was then
known as the new unionism, the organization of every
craft connected with a given industry into a single union.
He had no taste for theory at all, but made up for that by
a strong sense of justice, and a belief in his personal mission to lead men in combat, in all manner of struggles for
a better life, a little more dignity, a little more freedom.
He made no appeal to reason, advanced no theories, only
recited wrongs and outrages in angry tones, labor's wrongs

and Ireland's together. When men fought him, he lashed out not at their ideas but at their persons. When a single symbolic name could not be selected, he still knew how to make the contempt and hatred and anger seem personal. He never excoriated "the capitalist press," only a particular newspaper owner or editor who was the target of his wrath. For their part, his opponents and the hostile newspapers paid him in kind. He was a tough Irishman and they were tough Irishmen, and neither side was disposed to give quarter. But no matter how tough his methods of fighting, he knew how to elevate the feelings of those who listened to him. Sean O'Casey was to write of Larkin that he had brought "not only the loaf of bread but the flask of wine"—poetry and dignity and self-respect to the Irish labor movement.

He wanted to move things forward, not to get to any place in particular. No system or simple solution would ever satisfy him as final. In that sense he was never a socialist at all. Nor was he willing to settle for improvements; for him, the fight for freedom could never end. When John Redmond was willing to compromise the struggle for Irish freedom by settling for home rule within the Empire, Larkin said: "We are demanding [Home Rule] because of who we are; because it is in our very marrow; because of the men who died that we might live; because in a word we want Home Rule that WE MAY RULE OUR OWN HOME. But no man has a right to fix a Boundary to the March of a Nation; no man has the right to say to his Country, thus far you shall go and no further. We have never attempted to fix the Ne-Plus-Ultra to the progress of Ireland's nationhood, and we never shall."

The capitals, so to speak, were part of Larkin's style as they were of his oratory, a manner of making the big words resonant and emphatic. And so far as freedom was concerned, there was never a final settlement in that either, or in human dignity, only a series of steps on the road. In this sense Larkin was never a socialist at all because he did not believe in a socialist system complete in all its parts, any more than he did in a capitalist system. There were only varying degrees of exploitation and generosity, and workingmen would never be one whit larger or better just because of some change in the system without a change in their attitudes and behavior as well as in their rights and their dignity.

Larkin had many English, Scottish, Welsh, and Canadian friends. He accepted British trade union aid in the great dockers' strike of 1913, defying the pronouncements of Archbishop Walsh of Dublin in order to send Irish slum children to the homes of British workingmen, most of them low church dissenters or Christian socialists, to be cared for during the strike. Generally speaking, Larkin *omligated* every word that the Archbishop of Dublin said—omligate being one of his weird neologisms—but his Grace had to talk good sense and Christian charity or Larkin would have none of his advice or precept.

From boyhood, Jim was an omnivorous reader. That the books within his grasp might be on the Index made no difference. But they had to be full of spirit, brave and free and passionate; they had to be Christian in some sense, and strong for liberty or equality.

"How did I get my love of comrades?" he demanded of the testy Judge Weeks and the prejudiced jury in his trial in New York for "criminal anarchy." "Only by reading Walt Whitman," he responded. "And how did I get this love of humanity, except by understanding men like Thoreau and Emerson . . . and Mark Twain? These are the men I lived with, Your Honor, the real Americans, not the Americans of the Mart and the Exchange, the men who sell their souls for money and sell their country, too." The testimony did not endear him to the Judge nor recommend his case to his jurors.

His love of Irish freedom and of a decent life for the

underdog made a rebel of him in the slums of Liverpool and along its dockside. After building some organization among the Irishmen of England, he went to the mother-land of his spirit and began his efforts, together with Jim Connolly, to organize the workingmen of Belfast and Dublin. Connolly was the theoretician, having learned the doctrines of socialism and of "one big union" in America. Larkin was the agitator, the organizer, the fighter on the firing line. He never seemed to prepare a speech, being always ready with invective and his ad libs. Acoustics, whether of hall or roaring streets, were of no moment. His voice was strong and strident, and at climactic points turned to withering scorn or exultant roar. His great service was the organization of the Dublin strike of 1913 and when the police lined up to seek an excuse for breaking up one of his mass meetings, he looked them over and turning to his audience shouted, "Look at 'em, well-dressed, well-fed! And who feeds them? You do! Who clothes them? You do! And yet they club you! And why? Because they are organized and disciplined and you are not!"

To a British Trade Union Congress which he appealed to on December 9, 1913, for strike action in England to help his losing cause, when speaker after speaker had spoken in the negative, he began with the words, "Mr. Chairman, labor leaders, and human beings." They voted funds but no strike action. At another meeting in Scotland in response to a steady cry of "We want Larkin," the frightened chairman finally gave him the floor with the words, "You can speak, Jim, but na personalities," Larkin echoed his words, "Na personalities, Mr. Chairman, ye are not personalities at all, only things."

As the long Dublin struggle continued, a certain Captain White, Irish of course, came forward with a proposal for the formation of an Irish citizens' army to protect the workers' meetings, to buy boots and staves and food for them, to drill them as a matter of maintaining discipline. Larkin took up the idea as his own, and thus the Irish

Citizen Army was born. Sean O'Casey became its first Secretary.

Many a famous writer enlisted his services in the long and bitter strike. Besides O'Casey there was Padraic Colum, James Stephens, A. E., and even Yeats. As the strike petered out, gun running began for the Irish Citizen Army as well as for the opposing Carsons' Volunteers. For eight months the strike dragged on until all were weary, Connolly and Larkin at odds with each other, starving men and girls afraid to go to Transport Workers Hall and humbly plead for the few jobs that were not occupied by strike-breakers.

Yet the Transport Workers Union now had the solidarity of suffering, a tradition of struggle and self-respect, a martyred leader, a brace of heroes, and the remnants of the Citizen Army which survived the defeat and adopted as its banner the famous plough formed by stars on a blue background. When England and Germany went to war, Connolly felt that England's difficulty was Ireland's opportunity, and began to prepare for rebellion.

All through the strike Connolly had been eclipsed by Larkin's irascible oratory and he was tired of Larkin's headstrong dictatorial methods and uncontrollability. Connolly conceived of the plan of sending Larkin to New York to raise funds and arms from Germany's agents in America, and Larkin himself was glad to go.

His journey to America proved Jim Larkin's undoing. Like Antaeus his strength was great as long as he was in touch with his mother earth. In America he was out of his element. Though he was surrounded by a court of Irishmen, though he set up a journal called the *Irish Worker*, and founded a Connolly Club, he was somehow lost. He neither knew how to deal with the German agents that came with offers of guns and funds, nor with the Foreign Federations that made up so large a part of the American Socialist Party, nor with the Greenwich Village Bohemians who offered incense and incomprehension, nor with the materialism and atheism that was taken for granted in many of the intellectual circles. He missed the native soil. He missed the Dublin fray. His heart was in the struggle for Irish freedom to which he could now contribute so little.

Connolly took over the office of General Secretary of the Transport Workers Union, though, for prestige's sake, he retained Larkin's name on the letterhead. Shipping arms proved not to be feasible, and though Larkin raised large sums of money, they were mostly for the movement in America under whose auspices he spoke. In the controversy which followed on his return from an American jail to Ireland in 1923, the only sum credited to him as having actually arrived for the rebellion was £100. Yet it was certain that Larkin lived modestly as before and kept nothing for himself. What ate up the funds was the *Irish Worker*, the National Left Wing Council of the Socialist Party, the anti-war movement, the I.W.W., and the Connolly Club on 29th Street. He made several attempts to get back to Ireland during the war, even disguising himself to travel under false names, but his disguises were transparent, his huge, big-boned frame and strongly sculptured face could not be disguised, and his apparatus for shipping sailors did not work for his person.

In the American Socialist Party he was an explosive force that they could not manage. When the Left Wing Council of the Party formed in 1917, he got the highest vote of any of its nine candidates, yet he was not altogether at home in the Council either.

On November 8, 1919, a panicky national and state administration staged raids all over New York City and then all over the United States, raids on dance halls where left wing socialists, mostly foreign born, were celebrating the first anniversary of Lenin's seizure of power in Russia. Moving vans backed up at the dance hall entrances, and all the celebrants were herded into them and taken, in New York at least, for questioning by the Lusk Committee

set up to study "revolutionary radicalism." Virtually all
those who spoke English without a foreign accent and
seemed to have been born in the United States were released. The rest were held for imprisonment, photograph-
ing, and fingerprinting, the police line-up, and deportation. But the nine members of the National Council of
the Left Wing of the Socialist Party (or rather eight of
them, for they never laid hands on the ninth who was off
somewhere in a printing plant editing the *Communist
World*) were held for trial regardless of nationality or
accent. Jim Larkin was one of the eight.

When Big Jim arrived at the detention hall where the
frightened foreign detainees were huddled together, he
restored their courage by mocking at the police and jest-
ing at his plight. Archibald Stevenson, Counsel for the
Lusk Committee, tried his hand at interrogating Larkin.
But since he refused to tell the prisoner why he was being
detained nor what his legal rights were, Larkin met insolence with insolence to the point of a stand-off.

Ultimately, the eight members of the Council were
accused of having signed and sponsored the Manifesto of
the National Left Wing Council, and held, absurdly, under
the provisions of the Criminal Anarchy Law passed by the
New York State Legislature in the period of hysteria following the assassination of President McKinley by a crazed
anarchist.

Larkin conducted his own defense, and proved as
difficult to manage in the courtroom as on the street cor-
ner or in a union meeting. He claimed, I think rightly, that
he had never read the Manifesto of the Left Wing. It had
been written by John Reed and me, and then "corrected"
by Louis Fraina and certain members of the Russian Language Federation, who introduced many Bolshevik elements into what was originally a document of largely
native American radicalism. Larkin read it in the courtroom, sentence by sentence, repudiating its continental
and Russian orientation, pointing out that his own views

had developed out of British and Irish socialist traditions. There were phrases and thoughts on which he would not stand, nor had he had any part in its publication in the *Revolutionary Age.*

Larkin talked back to Prosecutor Rorke, as to an equal. And though he called the Judge (Weeks) "Your Honor," the judge got small comfort out of the tone in which he said it or the way Larkin handled himself in the face of constant threats of additional sentence for contempt of court. Rorke told the jury, a blue ribbon jury drawn from the world of business officials, "If you believe that this Manifesto means the overthrow of our Government by unlawful means, then sustain this indictment. . . ."

Larkin's summary speech was like an address to a mass meeting, heckled by Judge and Prosecutor but never thrown off balance by their objections and rulings. He told the story of his life as far as they permitted, cited the literature he had read and loved, and made a creditable defense in a technical sense as well.

"The Defendant claims," he said . . . "that he is not getting tried for any overt act; he is not getting tried for any attempt to commit an overt act; he is getting tried for within his mind focusing the ideas of centuries, and trying to bring knowledge into coordinate form that he might assist and develop and beautify life. That is the charge against the Defendant—that he preached a doctrine of humanity against inhumanity; that he preached the doctrine of order; that he preached the doctrine of brotherhood as against that mischievous, hellish thing of national and brute herd hatred."

"The Court has been stern with me," he said in summing up. "I have been a refractory person before the Court. I cannot preserve the ordinary procedure because I have not been trained in the way of the Court. The ways of the broad highways have been my ways, and I have never been encompassed by walls . . . so it may be tomorrow . . . that in the interest of this great Republic of

110,000,000 Americans, this individual will have to be put away for five or ten years."

An impartial judge would have directed an acquittal, an impartial jury would have found for the Defendant. But the jury found Jim Larkin guilty, and Judge Weeks sentenced him for "criminal anarchy," to a term of not less than five and not more than ten years. In 1923, Governor Alfred E. Smith declared that the trial had been conducted in a moment and in an atmosphere of hysteria and gave the prisoner an unconditional pardon.

While Larkin was out on $25,000 bail, which had to be in cash or Liberty Bonds according to Judge Weeks's ruling, and before he began to serve his term in Sing Sing and Dannemora prisons, he took a flying tour of the United States, no longer as a Communist Party member, but as a political prisoner raising funds for the defense of other politicals. When he got to the West Coast, I was living there and heard him address a huge meeting in San Francisco held under the sponsorship of the Irish Republican Army, the Hindu Gaddr (Freedom) Party, various aboveground and underground organizations run by the Communist Party, a well-known San Francisco open forum, as well as some thirty San Francisco trade unions. His address was as full of fire as ever, so that when he ceased speaking, the money came rolling in in response to his appeal for funds. A question period followed. An inveterate forum goer who was notorious in San Francisco for invariably asking the same question regardless of the subject of the lecture, innocently put to Larkin his pet question.

"Mr. Larkin," he said, "what about birth control?"

Big Jim, thinking an insult to his Catholic faith was intended, turned a fiery red, then, when the color receded and he found his tongue he answered: "It's a Gawd damned shame your-r-r mother-r-r didn't pr-r-actice it!"

That ended the question forever at San Francisco

forums. As long as I lived in the city, the questioner never reappeared at another meeting.

When the news of Jim's pardon reached Ireland, his Union Executive wired its congratulations and asked the date of his return. His answer was to send a cable asking for £5000 to be forwarded to him immediately to buy a shipload of food and clothing for the victims of "fratricidal strife" in Ireland.

A gulf opened between him and the new Executive who knew neither Larkin nor Connolly. He did not fit into the new mood of constructive unionism and building up of industry in the new Irish Free State, and his last years in Ireland proved to be anti-climactic, serving only to show how as a result of his prolonged absence, he had declined as a leader of Irish labor.

A war broke out between the Executive Committee and Larkin's followers, who seized Liberty Hall by direct action only to be ousted by action of the Irish courts. Larkin's trial this time was bedlam—oratorical appeals, insults to opposing witnesses, helpless quarrels with the Court. Reminded of his duty to "respect the Court," he roared, "I will respect the Court when the Court speaks the truth." Ordered to leave the courtroom, his parting shot was, "This may be a Court of Law, but it is not a Court of Justice." In his absence a verdict was found against him.

The Dublin nights were made colorful by his mass meetings, but his style of oratory invited libel actions that kept the town in an uproar. Yet he remained popular with the rank and file dockworkers, who often insisted that he represent them in negotiations.

In 1924, the Moscow Soviet invited Larkin to come to its sessions as a representative of the people of Dublin, but he found nothing there to attract him, nor could they see "their man" in this wild-hearted rebel. I met him then,

in the dining room of a Moscow hotel, where he was raising a series of scandals about the food, the service, and
the obtuseness of waiters who could not understand plain
English spoken with a thick Irish brogue. Once the usual
piece of horse meat in cabbage soup, tough as leather,
which was served as the main course and called *shchi,*
yielded to an unexpected delicacy, beet borshch. But
from Jim's table came the angry cry, "Ye can't make me
eat this blood soup!" The result was consternation. Another time, he was furiously yelling *milk* in various tones
and accents, which he wanted for his tea, which in Russia
was customarily served with lemon. He subsided, speech-
less, when I told the waiter that he wanted his tea *s molo-
kom,* nor could he perceive any difference between my
words and his. The climax came when Moscow tried to
tell Jim Larkin of his duty to "defend the Soviet Union in
the face of the war danger." "What God damned fool of
a general," he demanded, "would ever try to invade this
frozen land?" The Moscovites were glad when this eminent Dubliner returned to his native land.

In Ireland Larkin built himself a splinter union and
a political movement which won him elections to the
Dublin Corporation, and then to the Dail for a North
Dublin constituency in October, 1927. But because of
bankruptcy and his failure to pay his legal expenses on
his various lawsuits, he was not allowed to take his seat.
In 1937 he won the seat for North Dublin once more, and
again in 1943 and 1944. In 1944 he was seated, but he
proved to have no ability as a legislator in a changed world
to which he was now alien.

Later, one of his sons, James, became the leader of
his Union, and another, Denis, Lord Mayor of Dublin. In
his last years, mellowing a little and losing some of his
wildness, Jim served on the Dublin Trades Council, on
the Port and Docks Board, and in the Dublin Corporation.
The fire and the bluster had gone out of him. Though re-

spected now because of his gray hairs and his long record of service to Ireland and to freedom, he was still feared as a hot-tempered orator who might stray from the subject but never give quarter once in a fighting mood.

During a bitter blizzard on January 30, 1947, Jim Larkin died. Despite the cold and snow, the tumult of Irish crowds which he so loved surrounded the approaches to Saint Mary's Church on Hadington Road, Dublin, and the Civic Guards had to force a passage for his coffin. He lay in state in the church while those who loved him, and many who did not, passed the coffin where one could see the brown rosary beads in his hand, given him by the Archbishop of Dublin.

Big Jim Larkin had never really fitted into the Communist Party, but in the Catholic Church as in the hearts of humble Irishmen, he remained to the end. At his death, many paid tribute to his memory. It was then that Sean O'Casey spoke the famous words that Larkin had brought to the labor movement not only the loaf of bread but the flask of wine. The age of heroic struggle was over in Ireland, and James Larkin had outlived his time. He did not fit into the orderly, constructive, bureaucratized labor movement any more than he was suited to be a puppet of Moscow. But for all the tumult in his temperament and chaos in his action, I have no doubt but that the lot of the unskilled Dublin workingman and the docksider are better for his having lived among them and fought for them.

3

The Conversion

"Zwei Seelen wohnen, Ach! in meiner Brust. . . ."

I FIRST BECAME aware of Samuel Putnam through his translations from Spanish, Portuguese, Italian, French, and other tongues into English. "There is neither recognition nor monetary reward in translation," he once wrote. "It is probably a compliment when a translation isn't noticed." But his translations were so sensitive, so right, so amazing in the variety of languages and the range of taste, that I came to know his name and to think of Samuel Putnam as one of those rare writers whose genuine vocation is translation.

He had fallen in love with the languages and letters of foreign lands in his childhood in Rossville, Illinois. He learned his first words of German from a Bavarian shoemaker at the age of 9; read the forbidden Rabelais in a hayloft at the age of 12 and, the same year, began to study Latin and Greek; won a scholarship to the University of Chicago as a result of a translation from Latin while a high-school student; failed to take a degree there because of his ill health; studied at the Sorbonne from 1909 to 1914, made Paris his mistress, edited an expatriate literary review, wrote poetry, art and literary criticism, biography, literary history, articles on sexual pathology; and, handicapped by frail health, tubercular lungs, and other illnesses which kept him bedridden much of each day, he did over 50 translations of novels, plays, and poetry, including Rabelais, Aretino, Pirandello, Belinski (from the Russian), Silone, Cervantes, Huysmans, Cocteau, and the Marquis

de Sade. At 57, he began the study of Rumanian to ex-
plore yet another literature for America.

Early in 1944, I reviewed *The Road to Teheran,* by
the historian Foster Rhea Dulles, for the New York *Herald Tribune.* It was a history of the relations between
Russia and the United States from the time of Catherine
and the birth of our republic to the moment when Stalin,
Churchill and Roosevelt met at Teheran. Only the last
chapter troubled me because it was tainted with the Grand
Alliance illusions which boded ill for the planning of a
decent peace. I hesitated, then decided that the book was
so good that a polemical analysis of the last chapter would
be unjust to the work as a whole. I decided to say nothing
about the last chapter, concluding my review with the
words: "unreservedly recommended." Because of its time-
liness, the *Herald Tribune* took my brief review of a
scholarly book and, dressing it up with an imposing picture of Stalin, Roosevelt, and Churchill seated on the
portico of the Russian Embassy at Teheran, gave it the
entire first page of the Sunday *Book Review.*

A few days later, a friend sent me a clipping from the
Daily Worker. It was a literary column, apparently a regular feature of the paper. "Here," it said of *The Road to
Teheran,* "is one book we don't have to read, because it
was favorably reviewed by Bertram D. Wolfe in the *Herald Tribune.*" The column was signed *Sam Putnam!*

A few days later, my correspondent sent me another
clipping from the *Daily Worker.* This time, it was from
the "Letters from Our Readers" column. It contained two
letters that had every appearance of having been cooked
up in the office of the paper. The first praised the literary
columns of Sam Putnam, urging that they be reprinted in
pamphlet form to show writers and intellectuals the communist attitude toward culture. The second letter read:

So! Sam Putnam says that *The Road to Teheran,* by

Foster Rhea Dulles, is a book we don't have to read because it was favorably reviewed by Bertram D. Wolfe in the *Herald Tribune*. It's a pity Sam doesn't read the *New Masses*, for if he did he would find in the latest issue a warmly favorable review of two-and-one-half pages by Corliss Lamont.

The letter was signed: "Puzzled Reader." It must have produced a very puzzled Sam Putnam. Obviously, the party nabobs had decided to push the book because of the last chapter which I had decided to ignore. Sam Putnam had condemned a book without reading it because it had been favorably reviewed by a writer of whom he knew only that party leaders had attacked him. Thus, Samuel Putnam, the sensitive and conscientious scholar, was brought face to face with Sam Putnam, the party-line literary critic. The two were suddenly forced to confront each other. The resulting dialogue, inaudible to the spectator, puts an end to Act I of this little drama.

A week later, the Books Editor of the *Herald Tribune* sent me a new book to review. It was *Os Sertões,* translated from the Brazilian Portuguese of Euclides da Cunha under the title *Rebellion in the Backlands,* "with introduction and notes by the translator, Samuel Putnam."

It turned out to be a great book—to my mind, one of the two greatest books on sociology ever written on the American continent. Published in Brazil in 1902, it was soon recognized by Brazilians as *nosso livro supremo*—"our finest book." As I read it, I was inclined to pronounce it a *livro supremo* of the Americas. Written in a turbulent baroque prose always bordering on drama and poetry—"a monstrous poem of brutality and force," da Cunha himself had called it—and filled with Brazilianisms, regionalisms, Negroisms, Indianisms, and all the intensity of the human and geological inferno that was its setting, *Os Sertões* was a work to tax the skill, patience and artistry of the best of translators. My review exalted the book and praised translation and translator.

At that point, Daniel Bell, then an editor of *The New Leader,* now Professor of Political Science at Columbia University, took a small part in the drama. Under the heading, "Dilemma of a Literary Hatchetman," he told his readers the story of my review of the Foster Rhea Dulles book and Sam Putnam's reaction thereto. Then he cited my review of *Rebellion in the Backlands,* adding: "Here's another book we don't have to read because it has been favorably reviewed by Bertram D. Wolfe in the *Herald Tribune.*"

Here we let the curtain drop on Act II, with Sam Putnam and Samuel Putnam still engaged in a troubled internal dialogue.

For two years, Samuel Putnam labored over another great Brazilian classic, and early in 1946 he produced *The Masters and the Slaves,* a translation from the Portuguese of Gilberto Freyre's *Casa Grande e Senzala. Casa Grande* is the "big house" of the master, and *Senzala* the slave quarters. Freyre uses them as symbols to suggest the original cultural antagonism and social distinction between masters and slaves, blacks and whites, Europeans and Africans, over the span of three centuries, and the gradual closing up of that social distance by mating and inter-marriage and democratic class fluidity in the course of the formation of the Brazilian nationality and "cosmic race." The book is as vast as Brazil; the author broods over the birth of his land and people until he is "able to feel the life lived by our ancestors in all its sensual fullness."

As if to remind Sam Putnam of my existence, the publisher adorned the jacket of his new book with a quotation from my review of the earlier *Rebellion in the Backlands.* And the Books Editor of the *Herald Tribune,* thereby reminded that I had reviewed the other work, sent me *Masters and Slaves.* I ended my article:

I cannot close this review without a tribute to the translator. This is the second time that Samuel Putnam has made available to us a great Brazilian masterpiece that is at the same time a masterpiece in its genre and in the literature of our time and hemisphere. . . . In both cases, he has wrestled with an enormous vocabulary of Brazilianisms, Indianisms, Africanisms, and has given these masterpieces a style that closely approximates their originals, yet has comparable literary quality in our own language.

Curtain on Act III.

Thenceforward, fate willed it that Samuel Putnam's work should be continuously linked up with me and his name with mine. He translated a Brazilian novel, *The Violent Land,* by Jorge Amado; a Mexican novel, *Yo Como Pobre . . . ,* by Magdalena Mondragon; a brief history of Brazilian literature, and he wrote a survey of four centuries of Brazilian writing which he entitled *Marvellous Journey.* Each of them came to me to review.

At last, in the third year after our first strange encounter, he did a *Portable Rabelais.* This was a field in which I have no special knowledge, and here at last was a book which should not have come to my desk. But I received a copy all the same. On the flyleaf were inscribed the words:

> *For Bertram D. Wolfe,*
> *A Critic who has been much kinder to me than I deserve,*
> > *Samuel Putnam.*

I sent the giver a note of appreciation, telling him that I was especially moved by the inscription because I thought I understood something of the background from which it sprang. With that began a literary friendship, and, though Putnam found the journey from his home in Pennsylvania to New York too much for his strength, we got to know each other intimately through an occasional exchange of letters.

Here the little drama of the conversion of a communist might well end, but there is an epilogue.

Early in 1948, one of the editors of the Viking Press called me up: "Bert, we'd like you to read a new translation of *Don Quixote* and give us your opinion."

I protested that I was too busy with my own writing, that *Quixote* was too big a manuscript, that publishers did not pay readers enough for readings, that I was abandoning my Hispanic expertise and striving to become an expert on things Russian.

"But you don't have to read the whole thing. Read as much or as little as you please . . . a single chapter . . . a few pages . . . enough to make up your mind. You will be the judge. Printing costs are so high, and this book is so big, that if you say it is merely a good translation we will not publish; but if you say, 'This is the translation of *Don Quixote* that the English-speaking world has been waiting for,' we will go ahead with publication. Let your conscience be your guide as to what test passages you select and how much you read. For your report we will pay you a hundred dollars. The man has worked sixteen years on the translation. He quotes your strictures on other translations of Don Quixote in his preface. . . ."

"Who's the translator?"

"Samuel Putnam."

Once more, a capricious fate had linked our two spirits!

I read the manuscript with considerable trepidation. In his introduction, Samuel Putnam stated his translator's credo:

> To come to grips with the author's mind, with what he thought and what he really wrote . . . to present it with the greatest possible fidelity, clarity and simplicity . . . to attain a style which, like the original, shall be free of affectation, colloquial and modern without being flagrantly "modernized' . . .

combining textual fidelity with readable prose . . . to
overcome those obstacles that have inevitably been
erected by time and distance as precious antiques
need from time to time to be refurbished to bring
back the original luster. . . .

My report to the publisher, my congratulations to Sam
Putnam and, in due course, my inevitable review in the
Herald Tribune confirmed that these high and difficult
aims had been nobly carried out.

That autumn, it was Sam's turn to read and comment on a book of mine. In a letter to me, he spoke for
the first time of his conversion.

Others [he wrote] will do justice to *Three Who
Made a Revolution* as history and biography and
English prose. There is one aspect, however, that I
should like to mention to you which they will omit:
the cold, cruel but invigorating clarity it brings to one
who, like myself, knows what it is to have floundered
for a decade and more in the Machiavellian mazes of
the party line . . . only to be disillusioned in the end—
disillusioned and more than a little ashamed. . . . The
value of your book for those like me lies in the fact
that, by showing us the historical bases of our error,
it restores something of self-respect and affords the
basis for a new start. . . . I want to express my personal gratitude. . . .

In December, he made public acknowledgment of his
change of heart in a letter to *The New Leader,* in which
journal he professed to find the spirit that he needed:

a deeply rooted faith in a progressively socialized
democracy of our own type (by its very nature ever
subject to improvement) together with a truly liberal
attitude toward differing points of view and an intellectual spirit that for me had come to be summed
up in the words of the historian Charles A. Beard:
". . . *walk lightly. Things are not so simple.*" . . . This

comes as a great relief to one who, for nearly a decade and up to three years ago, out of misguided humility had forced himself to live in the stifling atmosphere of the party line with all its ruthless intolerance for the processes of the mind. . . .

On May 7, 1949, we finally had our first and only personal encounter. Accompanied by his wife, Riva, who was also his nurse, companion, secretary, comrade-in-arms, and mother of his only son, he made the difficult two-hour journey from Lambertville, New Jersey, his new home, to New York, to have lunch and spend a few hours in talk with my wife and me. Appropriately he asked us to meet him in the Gotham Book Shop on 47th Street, whose garden in the rear he had helped make famous by his lectures on the Latin literatures. I was deeply moved on contemplating his frail figure and realizing that this weak, tubercular man, who spent a good part of each waking day flat on his back, had managed to produce some nine or ten original books, hundreds of articles and poems, and fifty translations from perhaps a dozen tongues. Even then, he was full of plans for more translations and the study of fresh languages.

That autumn, I went out to California on a Hoover Library Fellowship to do research for additional volumes of my history of the Russian Revolution. Though I was there on a Slavic Fellowship, Sam wrote to the head of the Romanic Division about me, and I ended up with an appointment as Visiting Lecturer in Spanish Culture, giving a course in *Don Quixote*.

On January 16, 1950, Riva Putnam wrote me:

Sam died, unexpectedly and without warning, of a heart attack yesterday, just an hour after he had put his finishing touches on the Cervantes *Portable*. . . . He talked and planned with me until time for his nap, and he had lain down for only a few moments . . . he died that quickly. I am taking his body to his native Rossville, Illinois tomorrow. . . . I have wished

and wished that you were nearer so that you could
be there. . . . His dearest wish in case of death was
to have friends who knew him and his work deeply
speak for him, and he often said that the one he would
prefer above all would be you. . . .

I want only to add the impersonal fact that in 1946,
when the United States was badly in need of friendly
neighbors, as it is today and always, the State Department
sent Samuel Putnam, historian of Brazilian letters and
translator of Brazilian masterpieces, on an exchange pro-
fessorship to Brazil. He lectured on comparative literature
at the University of Brazil, made our own literature better
known to Brazilian intellectuals, was elected a member (I
believe the only Anglo-Saxon member) of the Brazilian
Academy of Letters, and was awarded the Brazilian Government's Pandia Colgeras Prize for literature in 1947. He
would have served with equal distinction as an ambassador
of good will in any one of a half-dozen other lands whose
literature and culture he did so much to make known to us.

I have often thought of his conversion that started
with a book review, and of the complexity of the human
spirit, as I have watched Congressional committees dealing with the youthful, or not so youthful, errors . . . or
dreams . . . of former communists. We might do well to
remember that the human spirit is fearfully and wonder-
fully made, and that a Wise Man once urged that, in things
of the spirit, more can be accomplished by coals of fire
than by bullying. In any case, our country is the richer
because Samuel Putnam lived in it, and in other lands,
from 1892 to 1950.

4

The Red
Queen Victoria

IN HER PRUDISHNESS, in the ethical nature of her socialist views, in her diminutive stature (she was less than five feet tall), in her dress, her love of old fashioned shawls and capes, in the longevity of her public life, there was something Victorian about Angelica Balabanoff. All in all, she was the most unlikely person to have become a close associate of the amoral Lenin, Zinoviev, and Radek —the most improbable of persons to serve as First Secretary to the Communist International. Yet, for several years, with the world in flames and Russia ploughed up by revolution and crisis, that improbable pair, Angelica Balabanoff and V. I. Lenin, worked together in such close collaboration that it was possible for Dr. Balabanoff to know Lenin as few have known him. In the end, neither succeeded in altering or influencing the other in the slightest; they parted company for good, each retaining a complex and critical respect for the other.

At the age of eighty-five the redoubtable Angelica wrote the last of several memoirs concerning V. I. Lenin, entitled *Lenin Visto da Vicino*, which was published by the University of Michigan under the title, *Impressions of Lenin*. It is a remarkable profile, really a double portrait, like a magnet with two opposing poles and magnetic lines of force running from one to the other. The one pole is Angelica herself, the other her chosen subject—as unlike each other as two persons in the international socialist movement of the first quarter of our century could possibly be. The combination of attraction and repulsion gives the double portrait a peculiar charge of energy, and a special life to each of the two poles. In addition, it provides an insight into the range of the spectrum of the socialist movement itself, from ultraviolet at one end to infrared at the other.

What brought these two so diverse personalities together so that for the years of World War I and the first years of Lenin's dictatorship they were able to work together in a common organization and—or so they imagined —in a common cause?

Angelica Balabanoff was born into a wealthy Jewish family on the outskirts of Chernigov, near Kiev, in the Ukraine, in 1878. Her father was a landowner and businessman, absorbed in his affairs, rarely intervening in the training of his numerous children. She was the youngest of sixteen children, only nine of whom grew to maturity. When she was born, all her older sisters were already married. Her mother was determined to make of this, her last daughter, a "fine lady." Surrounded by governesses who taught her many languages and the graces considered proper to a "fine lady," she was kept away from school and playmates, taught good manners, music, dancing, embroidery, and the propriety of charitable deeds.

It was the exercises in dispensing charity which started the lonely child on her way to socialism. She watched her mother commanding the servants and asked herself *why some commanded and others obeyed*. At the age of five she was taken to the poorhouse to dispense gifts, got the shock of having her hand kissed by a kneeling and grateful recipient, and responded at the first opportunity by kneeling and kissing the hand of the next to whom she gave alms. *Why,* asked her second question, *are some poor and some rich, some grateful to receive alms and some proud to give them?* Since neither mother nor governesses would or could answer these questions, she rebelled, demanding to be permitted to go to school like other children and find out, or so she fancied, the answers to the questions that were troubling her. This concern with the "poorest and most numerous class," to use the words of Saint-Simon, was always the real core of her socialism. To this concern she added a love of liberty, the first roots of which were nourished by her need to rebel against her mother in order to get contact with the world and humanity and make of herself what she wanted.

When the girl reached eleven, her mother gave up the battle of keeping her from school. Angelica had been taught only foreign languages but in secret was teaching herself to speak the language of the poor around her, so she passed her examination in Russian also. Trips with her mother to Switzerland, a proper thing for one who was to become a "fine lady," gave her her first glimpse of Russian students in exile. At the age of nineteen, after many stormy scenes and hysterics, she won the right to go to a university in Brussels, of which she had heard but vaguely, and to accept from her father's fortune only enough to travel third-class and "live like a working girl." She had to go without a blessing or a farewell from her thwarted mother. ("My last memory was to be her curse upon me.")

Angelica has spoken with nostalgia to her intimates about her girlhood home with its twenty-two rooms, its beautiful garden and orchard, the quiet provincial town and the lovely river flowing by, but all her life she has lived "like a working girl" in a tiny, barely furnished room, with a little table, a few shelves for her beloved books, a one-burner primus stove to make tea, a cozy to cover the teapot, a jar of jam to sweeten it, and on the table two or three of her beloved "ikons," a portrait of August Bebel, or Rosa Luxemburg, or Jean Jaurès, or Antonio Labriola, or as many of the men and women she admired as the little table of the moment might hold without interfering with the possibility of some guest and herself taking tea on it.

When Victor Serge met her in the middle twenties, he wrote:

> She lived now sometimes in Vienna, sometimes in its outskirts, carting her possessions, those of the eternal poor student, from one furnished room to another: the spirit-stove for tea, the small pan for omelettes, and three cups for her guests; together with the huge picture of Felippo Turati, the manly, glowing portrait of [the martyred] Matteotti, files of *Avanti*, the correspondence of the Italian Maximalist Party, and notebooks full of poems. Small, dark, and beginning to age, Angelica still led her eager militant's life which, with its romantic fire, was about three-quarters of a century too late. . . .

When I visited her in her little furnished room in a run-down hotel on the West Side of New York City, the scene was the same: the modest furnishings, the warm hospitality, the zeal and unflagging hopes, the notebooks of poems, the pictures of the fighters for her cause whom she had known and admired, a little unhappy that New York did not give her the same opportunity for activity as Rome or Vienna or Moscow, a little bewildered by the interest of the "American masses" in the World Series, but all else unchanged. As soon as the war was over and Mussolini fell, she hastened back to Italy, living in Rome in the same kind of room, with the same furnishings and pictures and poems, but with spirit revived because of the opportunity to work for the Democratic Socialist Party of Italy. And until 1964, in her middle eighties, she lived the same active life, a little slowed up, surrounded by the same favorite objects in the same unchanging room of a poor student.

When the nineteen-year-old Angelica left home and family to study in western Europe, she picked, on the basis of vague report, the Université Nouvelle of Brussels, not to be confused with the more solidly based Université Libre. The university had been built around the personality of Élisée Reclus, the noted geographer who was an exile from France because of his anarchism and his participation in the Paris Commune. At the university and at the People's House of the Belgian Socialist and Labor Movement all her teachers were either socialists or anarchists. She heard the greats of the Belgian Socialist Party, she attended debates on labor history and tactics, she foregathered with poor Italian and Russian emigrés. From them and from books she sought to find the answers to the two questions she had asked her mother and to which her mother had had no answers. Her rebelliousness became libertarianism, her compassion for the poor and suffering, equalitarianism. These moral positions were already part of her when she left home; what she sought now was a "scientific" underpinning for her moral attitudes, a proof that the nature of history and society were such that they must bring to pass the kind of world of which she dreamed.

From Brussels to Leipzig, to Berlin, to Rome she pursued her quest, acquiring her doctorate along the way, still seeking the "scientific proof" that the poor must not only be exalted and granted full human stature but were predestined by their very privations and plight to become the saviors of all mankind and the architects of a more humane society. That faith is the religious side of socialism, a faith which she acquired in the course of her studies and activities and which, as her latest work shows, possesses her still. That is what she means when she uses the word "science." To her that is the science of "scientific socialism," the sum and substance of her Marxism. The

greatest of her teachers was Antonio Labriola, who was
giving courses in philosophy and ethics at the University
of Rome at the turn of the century. Her favorite maxim is
neither from Marx nor Engels but from Labriola: "to put
knowledge at the service of the proletariat."

Thus from an ethical creed her beliefs grew into what
she called a "scientific conviction," and, in 1900, she was
ready to join the Socialist Party.

But which party? Angelica was a native of the
Ukraine, by citizenship a Russian. Yet the Russian movement, with its underground stratagems and deceits, its
bitter factional quarrels, its self-righteousness and unscru-
pulousness in battle with a rival faction, were not for her.
Her moral makeup was too simple and straightforward.
Her talents, which soon became evident, lay in open meetings, in addressing a moving word to multitudes. A gifted
linguist—she has written poetry in five languages and can
speak eloquently, as I know by experience, in six—she
could have functioned in any one of a half dozen continental socialist parties. She was at home with French,
Belgians, Swiss, Germans, Russians. Her demands were so
modest, her eagerness to serve so palpable and touching,
that she would have been welcome even in the most exclusive of them. After all, did they not all think of themselves as "internationalist"? And was not she in her diminutive self a kind of international?

The warm spirit of the Italian people and the dismal
and unprotected state of Italian unskilled labor in Switzerland combined to make her decision. She became a member of the Italian Socialist Party. Then she went to St. Gall,
in German-speaking Switzerland, where the majority of
the poorest laborers in the textile mills were Italian immigrants, at a disadvantage both in relation to their employers and their fellow unionists because they spoke no
German. She asked for a "job" in the Swiss Trade Union
Headquarters, an office, a desk, and no salary. It was the

pattern of party work she was to follow all her life. How she managed to live, even those of us who knew her best could never find out. Until the war she got a small stipend from her family, making up the rest of her needs by giving lessons in the many languages she knew. Later she rose to such posts in the socialist movement that a salary was assigned to her in spite of herself. But when I visited her in Rome in the early sixties, once more she had a little desk, an office, and no salary, in the headquarters of the Democratic Socialist Party of Italy, in charge of its work with women. Someone around the headquarters ran an occasional errand for her, or drove her in one of the organization's cars to meetings and to her eternal little "student's" furnished room. If a friend remonstrated with her, her answer was invariably to tell "how privileged my life has been, to have an opportunity to work unceasingly for the cause in which I believe."

Clearly then, to speak of Angelica Balabanoff and of V. I. Lenin is to speak of two opposing poles of the socialist movement. Her ideal was to serve the masses, his to manipulate them—both for the sake of socialism.

She was ill at ease with posts and honors and perquisites that go with being an official of any organization, trade union, political party, or corporation. He was a believer in the professional revolutionary, the full-time paid party worker, the importance of the official post, the Central Committee, the *troika* or triumvirate, the party leader, the infallible interpreter of an infallible doctrine. He fought for every delegate to a convention, used illicit means if necessary to get funds to bring his unquestioning followers to pack a Party Congress, tabulated the votes on every resolution, fought for hours and days to determine the makeup of the credentials committee, the exact order of business, the phrasing of every clause in every resolution. He served the faction first, she "the cause." She prized unity; he wrote to his followers: "Split, split, and again split"—until he had winnowed out the faction that would follow his views, which he was always so sure were right.

The Italian Socialist Party, the party Angelica Balabanoff knew and loved best, carried on a brave fight against Italy's involvement in the First World War, and then against the isolation of the Russian Revolution. But Lenin felt that the party was too large, too various, not homogeneous (or "monolithic" and pliable) enough to obey him unconditionally, hence he decided to split it. Without that split it is quite likely that Mussolini would never have been able to take power in Italy. Zinoviev, himself an unscrupulous tool of Lenin's, sent his most unscrupulous agents to attack its best leader, Serrati, politically from both the right and the left, and personally with slander. Serrati's crime was the same as Angelica would have committed: he refused to slander and expel old and well-loved moderate leaders of the Socialist Party like Turati and Modigliani, as long as they did not violate the decisions of the party majority. When Angelica Balabanoff protested to Lenin and Zinoviev, she was told: "We have fought and slandered him because of his great merits. It would have been impossible to alienate the masses [from him] without resorting to these means." When Serrati died the same Zinoviev who had directed the campaign against him wrote a long obituary emphasizing his incomparable services to the Soviet Union and the world socialist movement. As a dead man who obeyed the precept which the Germans call *Kadavergehorsam* (the obedience of a corpse), he was usable once more.

In a word, Angelica Balabanoff's approach to socialism was primarily ethical: she loved the downtrodden, the poor and suffering, and wished to alleviate their lot. She longed to believe in, and make them feel the dignity that came with their believing in, "their mission."

But Lenin's approach was partisan, factional, dogmatic, authoritarian, manipulative, organizational. He believed in the party's mission and his own. He sought to use the masses as the force behind the party battering ram. It was the dictatorship of the party that he meant when he said "Dictatorship of the Proletariat." Wherever Lenin and two or three unconditional followers were gathered together, there was the party. The party, given strength by the masses, would throw down the old, take possession of the ruins, and, still manipulating the masses, still dictating over society, would build the new. Even in the midst of war and revolution, Lenin never for a moment ceased contemplating the world as his chess board, never forgot to plan his next chess move.

His natural habitat was the underground, the factional group, the world of calculation and maneuver, the destruction of the reputation of whoever stood in his way. Her natural habitat was the open party, the mass meeting, the undifferentiated movement for a better world, the cause. No matter to which land Lenin was driven by circumstance, he neither learned its language nor its problems, nor participated in its life. Wherever he went, he carried with him an invisible envelope of the Russian underground. Angelica Balabanoff was active in the Russian, the German, the Austrian, the Swiss, and the Italian labor and socialist movements, and—to a lesser extent, for its ways were stranger to her and her stay here briefer—in the American socialist movement and Italian-American trade unions. Both she and Lenin in time came to be elected members of the International Socialist Bureau of the Second International and attended some of the same congresses. There Lenin worked behind the scenes, trying to influence more popular and better known figures to put some of his points into resolutions, trying to form an international faction akin to his faction in Russia. And there, on the stage, diminutive Angelica Balabanoff served selflessly as translator, seeming to grow in height as she spoke, rendering perfectly in all the languages of the Congress the eloquence of its famous orators, translating successively into French, German, Italian, until the applause was no longer for the eloquence and ideas of the man she was translating but for the perfection of her conveying of it in so many tongues. Where Lenin felt contempt for so many of the "greats" of the Socialist International, she felt the profoundest admiration and gratitude. With so many and such deep differences between these two opposite poles of socialism at the turn of the century, how did these two ever get together? How did they ever manage to work together in a single organization and a single cause from 1915 to 1921? The answer is to be found in two overwhelming events: World War I and the Russian Revolution of 1917.

In late August, 1914, the Socialist Parties of the World were to hold a Congress in Vienna. It would have marked the fiftieth anniversary of the founding of the Second International. But in the first days of August, Austria declared war on Serbia, Germany on Russia, France, and neutral Belgium, Russia on Germany and Austria, England on Germany. The Congress was never held. The new age had begun: the age of total wars and totalitarian revolutions.

For fifty years socialist orators had been assuring their audiences—and themselves—that the workers of all lands had a common cause, that they would never take up arms against their class brothers on the other side of the frontier, that their only enemy was within their own land, that socialist internationalism would prevent national war among civilized peoples. How many times had Angelica Balabanoff made such speeches herself and translated such sacred pledges for other orators! Now the German socialists voted the war budget and a *Burgfrieden* (civil peace) for the duration. The French socialists, more given to the poetic phrase, formed a *union sacrée* and entered into the government of their country. The Belgian leaders declared that they would never meet with a German socialist as long as there were German troops on Belgian soil. In land

after land, the socialists showed that they were French-
men, Germans, Englishmen, Belgians, before they were
socialists. With red cards in their pockets, uniforms on
their backs, and guns in their hands, stunned or stirred up
workingmen of France and Germany faced each other on
the frontier. The leaders were as much taken by surprise,
as much swept off their feet, as much stunned and grief-
stricken as their followers—many of them more so, for their
whole lives had been lived under the sign and the pledge
of international socialist solidarity.

But in every land there was some little handful who
were not swept away by the overwhelming tide, or, being
carried downstream, still sought to swim against the current. "We must redeem the pledge we have so solemnly
made, and redeeming it, redeem the honor of the International and restore across the frontiers the ties of brotherhood," they said.

In countries that were still neutral the socialist parties
had time to bethink themselves and issue the new call.
From all the warring lands first women, then the youth,
then men of military age, undertook the perilous journeys
to pledge themselves to struggle for peace and the renewal
of international ties. Angelica Balabanoff was one of the
leaders among them. And so, in his own way, was V. I.
Lenin—but he thought that to struggle for peace was
shameful and treasonable ("social pacifism" was the name
he found for the "deviation"). The thing to do was to
oppose the national wars, to smash the old International
as worthless, and to build a new "Third" or "Communist"
International, which would turn the imperialist war into
universal civil war. Angelica Balabanoff was attracted to
Lenin by the vigor of his opposition to the war between the
nations and the shameful betrayal of socialist internationalism. It would take years before she would understand
the differences that divided them.

In September, 1914, the Italian and Swiss Socialist

Parties, both from neutral countries, sought to draw together the remnants of the shattered International. Angelica went to Lugano on behalf of the Italian party.

In March, 1915, a Conference of Socialist Women
was held in Berne, Switzerland. Seven women came from
Germany, including Clara Zetkin, four from England, including Margaret Bondfield, one from France, three from
Holland, two from Switzerland, Angelica Balabanoff from
Italy, one from Poland-Lithuania, and four Bolshevik and
two Menshevik women from the Russian exile colonies
living in Switzerland. The Bolshevik women included
Krupskaya, Lenin's wife, Lilina, Zinoviev's wife, Inessa
Armand,[1] and Lydia Stahl. Lenin came personally to a
nearby tearoom to run his faction by remote control and
put across a special Bolshevik resolution. Inessa Armand
was his spokesman for the purpose.

This was the first conference to make a show of international socialist unity against war and for peace, and here
were Lenin and his mouthpieces insisting on disunity: a
vote of six against twenty-one in favor of disrupting the
International, against peace and for prolonging the war
into universal civil war. Clara Zetkin pleaded with Lenin,
but he was obdurate. During the course of several days of
argument and plea, she suffered a heart attack. At last a
compromise was reached. The general resolution would
be voted unanimously, provided the record of the proceed-
ings included the text of the special Bolshevik Resolution.
For the first time, Angelica glimpsed for a moment that
even world conflagration and misery did not make Lenin
forget to regard the human beings at war as pawns on his
great chessboard.

---

1. It is typical of the reticence or "Victorian" prudery of Angelica
Balabanoff that although she several times refers to the person of Inessa
Armand, who was living with Lenin and Krupskaya in a *ménage à trois*,
she never mentions her by name in her portrait of Lenin. When she writes
"I saw Lenin at the funeral of some one particularly dear to him . . . I
never saw any human being so completely absorbed by sorrow," the reader
will have to read the chapter on Inessa Armand to understand the roots
and full force of his sorrow.

A week later there was an International Youth Conference. Lenin was in the tearoom again, and Inessa Armand once more his spokesman, a little old for it, but with a youth credential.

On the initiative of the Italian and Swiss parties, with Angelica Balabanoff as the permanent representative of the Italians in Italy, an international socialist conference of neutral parties and anti-war minorities from the warring countries was called in the little village of Zimmerwald, near Berne, on September 5-8, 1915. Once more Lenin's representatives on the organizing committee tried to limit the conference to those who held to his view of opposing peace in favor of civil war and of forming a new leftist international, but the Italian party voted as did the organizing committee, to invite:

> all socialist parties *or their sections*, and all labor organizations which are *against any civil peace*, which adhere to *the basis of the class struggle*, and which are willing, *through simultaneous international action, to struggle for immediate peace*, which envisages neither forced annexations nor changes of state boundaries against the will of the peoples.

Lenin hastened to try to pack the conference with delegates adhering to his "left" view: "All this is *vertraulich* [confidential]," he wrote to Radek. "Promise not to speak of it to Grimm or Balabanoff or Trotsky or anybody!"

From those who could not come, he demanded proxies, which he made good use of. Across the shell-torn frontiers, through sentry lines, over mountain chains and through rivers, somehow thirty-eight delegates arrived from eleven countries. Most of them were from neutral lands, or, in various disguises as Poles, Letts, Latvians, etc., Russian emigrés. But there were ten from Germany, and two French trade unionists. Lenin managed to form a "Left Zimmerwald Group" of eight delegates. Quite naturally, the Russian from Italy, Angelica Balabanoff, who spoke so many languages and did all the translating as well as much of the preparing of the conference, became the secretary of the meeting and then of the International Socialist Bureau of the Zimmerwald Conference which issued out of it. Both Lenin and the "Social Pacifists" regarded her as the best and most trustworthy secretary they could get. There was the usual squabble between the Leninists and the rest, the usual compromise, the majority resolution adopted unanimously, with Lenin recording his own "chess move" for the record. The German and French delegates adopted a special resolution declaring, *"This War Is Not Our War!"*

Would the Zimmerwald Conference succeed in reconstituting a broad International on the basis of the struggle for peace? The question promised to be answered in the affirmative until, in March, 1917, the Tsar of Russia fell, after conspiracies against him even in the royal family and the general staff and a sudden mutiny of the reserve troops in Petrograd. This is not the place to tell the story of how Lenin got home across Germany with the aid of the German General Staff.[2] For our purposes it is sufficient to know that neither the allies of Russia nor the new democratic provisional government was willing to recognize that, the power apparatus of old Russia having broken down, the peasants in uniform could no longer be kept at the front. But Lenin, with his intense concentration on the chance of seizing power, was willing now to be for peace, if necessary for a separate peace with Germany. His turn to immediate peace brought the pacifist Angelica Balabanoff, thrilled by the liberation of Russia, to his side. And Lenin's awareness of the value of continuity in his chess moves made him claim, even as he split the Zimmerwald movement, that the new International he was forming was the

---

[2] It has been told, among other places, in Z. A. B. Zeman's *Germany and the Revolution in Russia, Documents from the Archives of the German Foreign Ministry*, London, 1958.

continuation of Zimmerwald. He made the secretary of the
Zimmerwald Bureau, Angelica Balabanoff, the secretary
of his new Communist International.

For the first time, day in and day out, she was forced
to observe the men he chose, the agents he used, the chess
moves he made, at first hand. Thus it was that she got "the
closeup of Lenin" which provides the Italian title of her
last book.

Lenin tried in vain to make his secretary of the Comintern into a Leninist and a Bolshevik. He tried to accustom her to unscrupulous agents and unscrupulous
methods; he sent her abroad with the instruction to "Spend
millions, many, many millions." She did not know how to
spend more than tiny, modest sums and could not dream
that she was to use millions to corrupt leaders and to
destroy those who could not be won.

When she understood, her whole being revolted at the
idea that this had been expected of her, or that this could
serve to bring about the better world she dreamed of.
Lenin and his agents sought to accustom her to the privi-
leges of a new privileged class, the élite that held power.
They did not know their Angelica. (For that matter,
Lenin, too, found privilege repulsive while all Russia was
starving; he would use it as a means of corruption and as a
raison d'état but he would not take such privilege for himself; in his heart, he could not help but respect Angelica's
incorruptibility even if it made her a poor instrument for his
purposes.) He tried in vain to accustom her to his single
moral, or amoral, principle, that the means justifies the
end, the end for the moment being the seizing, holding,
and extension of power in width and depth. She watched
with horror old socialists who had given their lives for
"the cause" slandered, put back into the same jails the
tsar had used, censored more ruthlessly and efficiently,
silenced, destroyed. Then she saw the Bolsheviks lead an
army of Asiatic recruits against the sailors and workers of

Kronstadt, when the Kronstadt communists demanded that the revolution live up to the promises it had made before Lenin took power. Finally, she had to watch Lenin splitting and destroying her beloved Italian Communist Party to extract from it a more pliable, if weaker, remnant.

Bit by bit, the first secretary of the Communist International began to go on strike. She refused to sanction unscrupulous agents and unscrupulous maneuvers. More and more, the chairman of the International, Zinoviev, had to do things behind her back. She began to find the false and demagogic speeches made to the Russian masses repulsive to her and suddenly ceased functioning as translator for official oratory. Subterfuges were used to get this troublesome moralist out of the way, into a sanitorium ("When all sick and weary women in Russia can go to a sanitorium, I will go"); to Turkestan, where cholera was raging and there were no workingmen to speak to; to the Ukraine as a deputy foreign minister of a foreign ministry without any powers. At last she went to Lenin and handed in all her documents, credentials, mandates, and asked for a simple permission to leave Russia with an identification paper which would get her past the sealed frontier.

In that last dialogue between two people who still had personal respect for each other there was deep sadness on both sides:

"Perhaps Russia does not need people like me. . . ."

"She needs them but she does not have them. . . ."

Angelica Balabanoff was probably the first communist in high place to break with the Communist International and go out in safety, without a campaign of personal slander. Years later, when Lenin was dead and his corpse the object of a cult, the Comintern began a slander campaign against her, and the Marx-Lenin Institute sent an emissary to beg from her the identity document Lenin had given her. She agreed, with one proviso: whenever they published the next slander, they must publish with it Lenin's last words concerning her. His identity document

1. JOHN REED—*Culver Service*

2. JAMES LARKIN

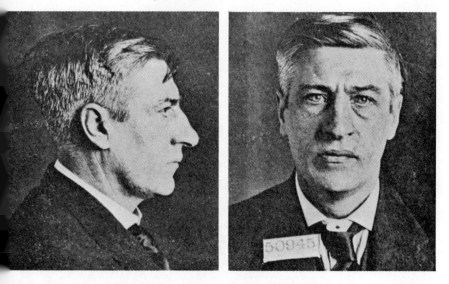

3. SAMUEL PUTNAM—*Etching by Joseph Stella, courtesy of Viking Press*

4. ANGELICA BALABANOFF

5. Yusuf Meherally

6. Rosa Luxemburg

7. INESSA ARMAND at the age of twenty

8. INESSA ARMAND in her mid-thirties when she met Lenin

9. ROMAN MALINOVSKY

10. MAXIM LITVINOV

11. LEON TROTSKY with DIEGO RIVERA

had asked "all institutions and individuals to give Comrade Angelica Balabanoff *every assistance required*" and it had called her "an old party member and the most outstanding militant representative of the Communist International." The proviso ended the campaign of slander.

Until her middle eighties, she continued her activities in the Italian Democratic Socialist movement of Saragat, now President of the Republic. Yet a note of deepening sadness crept into her letters to me as she saw the working class, the theoretical redeemer of itself and of society, dissolving into private persons each concerned with his job, his wages, his family, his motor scooter and radio, and not at all with brotherhood, the structure of society, the state of the world. She is too honest with herself not to realize that her dream has failed to come true, and that the lowly and humble to whom she has given her life are showing themselves to be self-centered, egotistical human beings not disposed to sacrifice the fruits of victory to "the cause." No matter how often she has protested in her letters that her life has been privileged in that it has served a noble cause, it is only too clear that "the lady doth protest too much."

Not long ago, she wrote her epitaph, which tells the tale of her disillusion:

> J'ai cherché la verité
> Et je l'ai adorée
> C'est à elle que j'ai immolé
> Ce que je suis et ce que j'ai été
> Je meurs oubliée . . .

As poetry it is not much. But as an epitaph it is the story of her disillusionment.

From Ivan Matteo Lombardo, I have received an account of her present state in her later eighties:

Sometimes she looks fine and appears to be still lucid and still fit for logical reasoning, and some times she lapses into a state of absent-mindedness and blurred reasoning. She has been taken to a village on the outskirts of Rome, situated at an altitude of 1,200 feet, where she is boarding with a private nurse, her board being paid by the Democratic Socialist Party which she served so long and well. In her room hangs Big Brother Togliatti's portrait, which she has not noticed or she would have the creeps. It is hard to find a nurse or a hostel there which is not pro-communist. She seems to be happy that evenings people visit her host and join in singing *Bandiera Rossa* (Red Flag). Nothing appears sadder to me than to see Angelica pleased to listen to people singing the communist anthem, whose aim is the destruction of the freedom for which she has fought all her life. She nurses fears about the Great Shadow and the Beyond, but we all try to divert her. Certainly, the day she will pass away will be one of bitter sorrow and mourning for us: an era closing and a moral institution passing away.

POSTSCRIPT

WHILE this book was on the press I received a letter from Angelica Balabanoff. She is well again and has rented another little "student's room" in Rome. A merciful forgetfulness has made the year of breakdown seem but a little moment during which "my nervous system was a bit disobedient." She has written an article for May Day on how today's workers should be addressed concerning socialism, and, at eighty-seven, has notified her party that she is ready for another lecture tour.

5

Gandhi versus Lenin

Memories of Yusuf Meherally

BORN ON SEPTEMBER 23, 1906, Yusef Meherally was ten years younger than I. He was born a Mohammedan, and owed much of his training to Mohammed Ali Jinnah, in whose offices he studied law. But when Jinnah began his break with the Indian Congress Party and his attempt to found a separate Mohammedan nation of Pakistan, Yusuf sided with Gandhi, whose disciple and friend he became. He founded the Bombay Youth League in 1928, organized the boycott of the Simon Commission on Indian autonomy because he demanded complete freedom, became General Secretary of the All-India Youth Congress, Secretary of the Independence of India League, one of the founders of the Congress Socialist Party adhering to the Indian National Congress, and then its General Secretary.

I first met Yusuf Meherally in the nineteen thirties at the home of V. F. Calverton in Greenwich Village, from which Calverton edited the *Modern Monthly*. Yusuf was dressed then in a close-fitting grey linen coat of Indian cut with standup collar, and wore a Gandhi cap. He seemed slight and frail, but full of vitality. Writers kept coming

and going all afternoon on Yusuf's request and at Calverton's invitation.

I forgot about Yusuf until he reappeared in the United
States in the winter and spring of 1946-47. He had served
a term in a British jail in India, gone through a prolonged
hunger strike, and been elected Mayor of Bombay on the
Congress Socialist ticket five days after his release from
the Lahore Central Jail.

Yusuf was suffering from a bad heart, and his doctors
had given him stringent orders to rest. He had taken a
room at the same hotel (the Duane) as Louis Fischer then
lived in, and Fischer was inviting to his suite all the writers
and other public figures Yusef wanted to meet. When he
found them interesting enough, Yusuf invited them to his
own little room, where, lying in bed, he would spend hours
in ardent conversation and exchange of opinions on all the
innumerable questions of philosophy, politics, history, art,
and ethics which interested him.

The circumstances of his wanting to see me touched
me deeply. "One of the tasks I was given when I set out for
America," he told me, "was to bring you greetings from my
cellmates of Lahore Central Prison. We spent many happy
years reading your *Portrait of Mexico*. We read it, studied it,
and discussed it together. I have been to Mexico where I
saw the originals of Rivera's paintings and frescoes which
you used as illustrations for your book. I have come to
thank you on behalf of myself and all my fellow prisoners
for the pleasure and enlightenment you provided us with
in prison."

"But how did you get my book in Lahore?" I asked.

"We had no decent books to read in prison," Yusuf
responded, "so I asked the jailer to lend me copies of the
Old and New Testaments. He refused, saying, 'You are a
Mohammedan, you may get the Koran to read if you wish,
but not the Christian Bible.

" 'If you do not give me your Bible to read,' I told him, 'I shall go on a hunger strike, and so will all my friends and fellow prisoners. The strike will not end until we get the Bible.'

"The hunger strike began and all my comrades in prison joined me. In a few days the jailer began to worry about our fasting and went to consult his superiors. They told him: 'This is impossible. We cannot let the world know that men are starving themselves to death because we refuse to let them read the Holy Bible.'

So the jailer came to me and said: 'O.K., here is the Bible.'

" 'It is too late now,' I responded. 'We will not call off the hunger strike until you agree to get us all the books we want for study while in prison.' He went away and the hunger strike continued. A few days later he came again and asked for a list of books we wanted to read. We put our heads together and made out a list of everything we had always wanted to read and had had no time for.

"After I left New York the first time I met you, I went down to Mexico and saw the beautiful paintings being done on the walls of the communal buildings by Diego Rivera, Oroczo and other great Mexican painters. Then I heard of your book dealing with the Mexican Art Movement and with Mexico. I wanted to read it, so I put it on the list which we handed the jailer. There were many other books we wanted and the authorities had great difficulty assembling them. In the end we got every book which was on our list, including yours. Your book was all I had hoped for. We not only read it, but studied it and discussed it and discussed all the questions it raised. That is why I have come to give you the thanks of all of us for the happy hours you gave us in our prison cell."

I gave Yusuf the books I had written since his prison days, among them my first biography of Diego Rivera[1] and

[1] I have recently done a second, *The Fabulous Life of Diego Rivera,* 1963.

my *Three Who Made a Revolution*. He, in turn, gave me
copies of his own writings, both books and pamphlets.

Though his bad heart had grown steadily worse, his
mind never slowed for an instant. I took the liberty of urging him to do more writing and less traveling through
India, less speaking at mass meetings and less of the other
things that were obviously taxing his frail body beyond its
powers. Even his incessant zeal to talk with people and to
question them was visibly draining his strength. He had
become so frail that his spirit seemed to shine through his
diminishing body like a wild bird beating its wings against
a cage.

I persuaded him that summer to join my wife and me
in Provincetown, at the tip of Cape Cod. There he took a
room at the Colonial Inn and spent most of the time in bed
with the windows shut tight because he was catching a
succession of colds which put an extra strain on his heart.
But whenever the weather was fine, and his health a trifle
improved, he visited the local artists and writers and entered again into the interminable discussions of all the
things on his mind. He loved the sand dunes, the pine
forest and the sea, but was not strong enough to plod
through the sand to reach them.

One day I arranged to take him in a station-wagon
with partially deflated tires to enable it to run over the
sand dunes. In it we toured the entire tip of the Cape,
both the inner shore of the great Bay and the outer shore
of the Atlantic Ocean. When we reached the extreme tip
of the peninsula I explained to him that it was known as
Race Point because a great tide raced around it where the
waters of the Atlantic Ocean and the waters of Massachu-
setts Bay came together.

"Would you stop here for a while?" he asked shyly.
We stopped and he walked down to the point where ocean
and bay waters met, took off his sandals, and waded into
the swirling waters. When he came out his face was lit up
with an expression of happiness that I had not seen before.

"We Indians believe that every confluence of waters is a sacred place," he explained to me.

I realized then that in his spirit was a blend of socialist internationalist philosophy with the ancient faith of his own people. His reaction had not been Moslem, but Hindu, and that impulsive action gave me a fresh and deeper insight into his mind.

From Yusuf I learned the story of Minoo Masani's break with the Congress Socialist Party and of the popular front experiment between the Congress Socialist Party and the Indian Communist Party. As a student of the International Communist Movement, I was familiar with the story of these popular fronts and united fronts in many lands but there was something unique in the Indian scene which made the experiment there turn out differently.

During the early thirties, after Hitler came to power, Stalin made several vain attempts to come to an understanding with Hitler. When these failed and the Anti-Comintern Axis developed, Stalin became alarmed and made one of his sudden turns to seek support in the League of Nations (which until that moment he had been calling "The League of Bandits"). At the same time, he made an alliance with France in the Stalin-Laval Pact, and the great drive for a popular front with Socialist and Democratic Parties. Up till then, the socialists had been called "social fascists," and democracy and socialism were "the main enemies." Now the Communist Parties offered the "hand of brotherhood" to all progressive, liberal, democratic, and socialist parties. Many of these were deceived, infiltrated, and later disrupted by this maneuver, which lasted until Stalin betrayed his democratic allies by signing his pact with Hitler.

Yusuf and the Congress Socialist Party of India were taken in by the fair words of friendship and not only accepted the communists into their ranks but helped the Communist Party to enter into the Indian National Con-

gress. The Indian communists were under secret instructions to penetrate and try to capture the Congress Socialist
Party, and above all, to discredit and destroy Mahatma
Gandhi. The Indian socialists, Meherally among them,
were as candid and unsuspecting as the socialists of other
lands. Yet they proved to possess an antitoxin which saved
them from destruction.

The only person, according to Meherally, who sounded
a note of warning that the communists were not morally
fit to enter the Socialist Party or the Indian National Congress was Minoo Masani.[2] "Minoo was in jail with the rest
of us at that moment," Yusuf told me. "We spent long
hours, and days and nights, trying to convince him, but we
did not succeed. Minoo insisted upon resigning from the
Congress Socialist Party if it accepted the communists
into its ranks. When we failed to convince him, we decided
to help him make his letter of resignation a really worthy
document. All of us had a hand in helping him with an
explanation of his reason for breaking with us."

Again, I realized that Indian socialism had some
strange quality missing from political life in other countries for I had never heard of a factional controversy in
which members of one faction tried to help the spokesmen
of another faction to put their position as clearly and
worthily as possible. I was mystified as I listened and pon-
dered what this strange ingredient in the Indian spirit
could be.

"Minoo was right, of course, although we did not
know it then," Yusuf continued. "Sometime later when I
got out of prison I discovered that the Communist Party
was guilty of double dealing and had constituted itself as
a hostile conspiracy within our movement. They kept up a
faction of their own, slandered our movement and its
leaders, secretly worked for the defeat of some of our candidates in the elections, made undercover alliances with

---

[2] Now a member of the Lok Sabah (Indian parliament) as a spokesman for the Swatantra (Freedom) Party.

opponents of socialism against us. Finally someone brought
me copies of a secret communist circular which they had
sent out to their members, giving instructions to support
reactionaries against Congress socialist candidates in certain districts. I called a number of the top leaders of the
Communist Party faction within our ranks to come to
visit me and I accused them of moral duplicity. Their
answer was a barefaced denial. Thereupon I took out a
copy of their circular and said: 'How do you explain this?'

"I was alone with their leaders; they snatched the circular out of my hand by force. 'Are you such fools' I asked,
'that you think that you can undo a moral crime by destroying a document? Do you think I am such a fool as to trust
you after this has come into my possession? Naturally I
have other copies in a safe place. You have proved unworthy of membership in a socialist movement. You have
proved unworthy of membership in the Congress Party
and you have proved unworthy of the moral principles of
Gandhiji. What you aim at is power for your Moscow masters. What we aim at is the freedom, the well-being and
the regeneration of our people. You and we cannot travel
together for our roads diverge. I give you one week to
withdraw all your members from our Party or we will
expel every one of them.'

" 'We will not give up the Congress Socialist Party,'
they answered. 'It is our Party now. We belong to it and
we will have control of it in a showdown.'

" 'I give you one week to withdraw,' I responded, 'or
we will expel every last one of you. It will be more honor-
able if you resign, for your continued membership in a
party you do not agree with dishonors you and us. But if
necessary we will expel you.' "

Once more I realized that it was some strange principle at work in the Indian Socialist Party which saved
them from the deadly vacillation of socialists and liberals
in other lands.

"Our National Committee," Yusuf continued, "sent

circulars to all our branches and locals and provincial committees throughout India, exposing the whole affair and directing the immediate expulsion of all known communists and all those who had sympathized with them, voted with them, fellow-traveled with them, or joined in any way in their conspiracy.

"'Do not be afraid to commit an injustice,' he wrote. 'If anyone is wrongly expelled, he will find it easy to prove his good faith and can be reinstated, but if any morally corrupting element remains, it will corrupt our party.'

"Within the time limit set by us, our Party was purified," Yusuf concluded.

"How many sections, branches, locals, and provincial committees did you lose as a result?" I asked, remembering how many parties were wrecked by such splits.

"We had no serious losses," he replied, "because the moral principle on which we acted was clear to our membership."

Suddenly I knew the answer. It was the influence of Gandhi within the Congress Socialist Party which had immunized it against the moral corruption of the communists. However much the Congress Socialists differed with Gandhi and he with them, they felt a kinship of moral purpose and therefore they were close together in the questions which mattered most. No other party anywhere in the world suffered such insignificant losses as the result of this unhappy experiment of working together with the communists.

I never heard Yusuf speak at any length of Nehru or Patel, but he talked frequently to me of his earlier relations with Mohammed Ali Jinnah, who had been his patron, and of Mahatma Gandhi, with whom he had had arguments on industrialization and socialism and other topics but for whom he felt the love of a son for a father and of a disciple for a revered master.

Though Yusuf was a Mohammedan and owed to

Jinnah much of his early training, when Jinnah broke with the National Congress Party and began his movement for a separate Pakistan, Yusuf remained loyal to India and the Congress Party.

He spoke of his former master, Jinnah, in tones of resolute rejection, but without bitterness. On the whole, Yusuf preferred to talk of things which inspired his enthusiasm rather than matters which he felt called upon to condemn.

Only when he spoke of the negative aspects of British rule in India, and of the monstrous moral corruption spread by the Stalin regime among intellectuals and workers, did I ever hear him become eloquent about matters he opposed.

On British rule in India, he was tireless. When he learned that I had spent much of my adult life working with the Indian Independence Movement in the United States, he found a fresh reason for closeness to me.

I told him stories of an earlier generation of Indian independence fighters whom I had known in the United States. During World War I, some had tried to get arms and help from Germany but their movement had been unsuccessful. Others had tried to work for Indian independence by influencing American public opinion, which in general has always been anti-imperialist.

The great test of America came when contrary to her whole tradition she engaged in a brief imperialistic spree in Latin America during the first two decades of the twentieth century. By the time Yusuf came to the United States, we had withdrawn our troops from all the Central American Republics, and the "Good Neighbor Policy" had completely replaced the "Big Stick" policy which had briefly marked our attempts to establish "order" in the turbulent Central American republics and to secure the approaches to the Panama Canal. Yusuf found the United States its old anti-imperialistic self and free from even a

shadow of controversy on the matter. He also found a
sympathetic ear in every circle into which he entered when
he spoke of Indian independence.

Yusuf plied me with questions concerning earlier
Indian independence fighters who had found refuge in the
United States and, unable to return to their homeland,
were dying in lonely exile on the West Coast of this country or in Mexico, with no prospect of ever seeing India
again. I was particularly close to a group of Sikhs who
lived in California and who had founded an Independence
Movement known as the Hindu Gadir Party, for in the
early twenties I had edited a newspaper partly owned by
the San Francisco Labor Movement and partly by the
Irish Republican Movement and the Hindu Gadir Party.

In turn, Yusuf told me much about the earlier British
rule in India, about the great textile industry which India
possessed when the British came and how the British
crushed it in part by competition from cheap Manchester
textiles and in part by brutal laws against native spinning.
Some of the stories he told me about ordinances which
provided for cutting off the fingers of people who insisted
on continuing their spinning and weaving were new and
startling to me in spite of my life-long concern with Indian
independence.

I did not know whether to believe those stories or not,
but I realized that Yusuf's picture of a once great Indian
textile industry must be a true one, for my philological
bent taught me to notice that many of the words for textiles in the English tongue came from India; madras, cal-
ico, cashmere, and the like. Thus the frozen history of
language bore partial witness to the truth of his incredible
words. He instantly added my insights from linguistics to
his arsenal of arguments in his talks to other Americans.

When England finally decided to withdraw from
India, I watched Meherally's bitterness ebb away. There
was no rancor in him. Thenceforward he talked very little
about British crimes in India, though he had spent much of

his life in prison because of British rule. Now he spoke rather of the good things the British had contributed to Indian civilization and culture, above all the sense of justice and the safeguarding of individual and civil rights that are inherent in the British tradition. He jested about the fact that in the vast sub-continent of India there were so many peoples and dialects that often the only common language in which Indian intellectuals could communicate with each other was the "language of the oppressor." That language, he told me, opened to the Indians a great literature and tradition which might be used to enrich their own.

I teased him about the "British sense of justice" which had kept him in jail so long. He answered in deep earnest: "Even while they oppressed us, they were uncomfortable about it. A hunger strike in a British jail could get me the Bible, or your book or other works to read. In Hitler's jails or in Stalin's it would only have gotten me before a firing squad. Gandhi's whole code of non-violent resistance to the evil of foreign rule was predicated on the unspoken assumption that the English had a better nature to which we could appeal. In the land of blood purges and concentration camps that Stalin has built to sully the name of socialism the great organized campaigns of non-violent resistance to evil could never have gotten started. If Gandhi had been in the Soviet Union, he would have disappeared forever from view after his first word of protest. The English at least felt that they had to report his defiance, even while they ridiculed it and imprisoned him. And they were always terrified lest he die in one of his protest hunger strikes. That is why he taught us to hate the evil things the English did but not to hate the English or ever despair of their regeneration or our own."

On one occasion I told Yusuf the story of my relations with Sam Putnam (see Chapter 3, "The Conversion"). After I had completed the story, Yusuf plied me with questions, trying to elicit more and more details of the spiritual conversion Putnam had undergone, like a child

trying to get more details of a story he has enjoyed. When
I had finally exhausted every aspect, Yusuf said, "Now
start all over again from the beginning, and don't leave
out anything."

"But why, in Heaven's name? You've heard it all. It
won't be any different, and I can't add another thing."

"This time I want to memorize it," he told me, "so that
I can tell it to Gandhiji just as you told it to me. He'll
love it."

I had to start all over again and Yusuf wouldn't let
me leave out a single detail.

As he talked to me about Gandhi, I began to realize
that there was a warm bond of affection and good-
humored intimacy that bound Yusuf to him in a relationship that was compounded of father and son, master and
disciple, friend and friend, in unequal parts. They had
obviously argued much, too, for Yusuf told me of Gandhi's
reservations about the class struggle aspect of Yusuf's
socialism and the socialist habit of treating some classes
as virtue incarnate and others as incarnate evil. The dogmatic, violent, amoral side of Yusuf's socialist creed had
been tempered by Gandhi's philosophy, while Yusuf had
his reservations on the "home-spun" aspects of Gandhi's
economics. But these were superficial differences. In their
hearts there was a tie of common moral principle and deep
affection, and the warm bond that links a devoted disciple
to a great teacher.

It was at this time that I told Yusuf about a change
of heart that I had undergone in my attitude towards
Gandhi as an Indian leader. It was during World War I
that I began to befriend the various Indian independence
fighters whom I met in New York, San Francisco, and
later in Mexico. In keeping with our tradition as a rebellious British colony that won freedom through revolution, I
supported all Indian efforts to secure independence

through revolutionary action. Nor was I alienated by the fact that some Indians sought support from our World War I enemy, Germany, for had not we ourselves received help from England's enemy, France, in our struggle for freedom?

Suddenly, I became aware of the existence of Mahatma Gandhi, as the movement he headed, or rather inspired, began to dwarf and absorb all other independence efforts. But then, as suddenly, in the early twenties, as Gandhi's movement seemed to be gaining irresistibly in numbers and power, I learned that he had called off the non-cooperation and resistance movement because he feared that it was getting out of hand. Living as we did more than half way around the world, we got no real explanation of this suspension. I formed the opinion that Gandhi had become a British puppet or a traitor to India's cause, and so I wrote in our press.

But as the years passed and I watched the ebb and flow and long range growth of the movement for Indian independence and regeneration under Gandhi's leadership I came to realize that I had been wrong about him. He had a profound knowledge of his people and their spirit, their weaknesses, and their possibilities. His conception of resistance to evil included the evil latent in his own people. He not only wanted to help them to be free but to help them to be worthy to be free. I became absorbed in his masterful sense of timing, and of the strategy and tactics of the double struggle for freedom and regeneration in which he was engaged. Gestures which at first had seemed silly to me—the home spinning and the march to the sea to scoop up a ladle of sea water and evaporate out the salt—I soon realized were profoundly symbolic and brilliantly conceived to mobilize his people, stir their spirits, and dramatize the struggle for freedom. I now saw that he was creating a ritual for his struggle and was striving to convert his people's belief in him into a belief in themselves. Thus he sought to prepare them for independence,

unify them, chide and restrain them when they were attracted to means unworthy of the ends they sought. How
badly they needed this type of leadership was demon-
strated by the terrible eruption of communal struggles at
the moment that freedom was attained. I made acknowledgment in my writings that I had been wrong about
Gandhi and that he was one of the few truly great men of
our time.

Yusuf was quite moved when he learned that I had
publicly acknowledged my erroneous estimate of Gandhi.
When Gandhi's birthday came in 1947, Yusuf came to my
home and presented me with a Gandhi birthday gift. It
was the lovely limited edition of the birthday tribute to
Gandhi printed on Gandhi's 75th Birthday. Yusuf had
sent all the way to India for it and on the fly-leaf he wrote:

> *For Ella and Bert Wolfe*
> *With affection and admiration*
> *Yusuf Meherally*
> *2nd October, 1947*
> *On Mahatma Gandhi's 78th Birthday*

It is one of the most cherished books in my library,
and into its pages I have inserted one of the photographs
of Yusuf taken in New York before he left. (It is the photo-
graph which is reproduced here.)

When Yusuf left Provincetown on the beginning of
his return journey to India, I helped him pack his bags
and was shocked by the massiveness and weight of his
baggage. He had accumulated hundreds of books, magazines, and manuscript articles, including some of mine,
which he intended to try to publish in India. He had had
too much baggage when he came. Every Indian, it seems
to me, carries too much baggage. Perhaps because, unlike
us, they are accustomed to many servants and human
labor power for personal service is cheap and plentiful in
India. But Yusuf's bags were laden far more than any

others with the dead weight of books. They contrasted strangely with his frail slight person. With his bad heart, he could not lift the lightest of his bags. It was as if he had tried to pack all our art, all our literature, all our culture, and all the mementoes of all the men and women he had known and the places he had seen into his baggage to take them all back with him to India. I secured the help of three men in and around the Inn, and the four of us managed to get the slight Yusuf and the massive baggage into a single cab.

My last words to him were an earnest admonition that he slacken up on his party work, his endless journeys and speeches and endless giving of himself to all and sundry. I urged him to conserve his strength and to communicate his thoughts henceforth through books and articles.

He half promised, but then he began to talk of the great eagerness of the Indian masses to hear and learn and the great need to teach what one could. "How can I deny myself to any one" he asked, "at any place or at any hour? There is so much to be done. And there is such joy in doing it."

I was not surprised when in 1950 mutual friends wrote me from India that Yusuf's frail heart had ceased to beat. He had given it to his people to the very end.

Yusuf Meherally left so profound an impression on so many people that the mention of my friendship with him to almost any new arrival from India serves as a credential. People come and seek me out because they have heard that he was my friend. And I am sure that if I ever get an opportunity to visit the land of which he revealed so much to me, his name will serve as my passport.

PART TWO

6

"The Last Man in the German Social Democratic Party"

ROSA LUXEMBURG and V. I. Lenin were born in the same year, 1870, and their lives were destined to cross at many points. Though they were both called "revolutionary" socialists, their diverse temperaments and their differing attitudes on the nature of socialist leadership, on party organization, and on the initiative and self-activity of the working class kept them poles apart. Among Rosa Luxemburg's best-known works are sharply critical appraisals of Lenin's penchant for personal dictatorship over his party, the dictatorship of his Central Committee over its locals, and the dictatorship of his party and its leaders over the working class and society as a whole. These critiques from Rosa Luxemburg's pen are among the most important works to have come out of the Socialist International, for, without ever using the word or the concept "totalitarianism," Rosa Luxemburg had a prescient feeling for the totalitarian potential in Lenin's views. Today, as we look at the party and the state which Lenin founded, we can no longer doubt that in this controversy Rosa Luxemburg was prophetically right.

Most of the political life of Lenin and Luxemburg was lived out in the old pre-war Second International, founded in 1889, which collapsed in the holocaust of war in 1914. That vanished world of international socialism possessed no more original, ardent, dynamic, and attractive figure than Rosa Luxemburg.

She was born in an "enlightened" Jewish merchant's family in the small town of Zamosc, in Russian Poland, near the Russian border. (Like so many of the self-constituted socialist leaders, or would-be leaders, of the working class, neither Lenin, whose father had earned hereditary nobility and whose maternal grandfather had land and peasants, nor Luxemburg, whose father was a well-to-do merchant, was of proletarian origin.) Her education she acquired in Warsaw, where her family moved when she was three years old. To say then that a Jewish family was "enlightened" was to suggest that it had broken out of the circle of ghetto culture and traditions and absorbed the general culture of the country. Rosa's parents were at home in Polish, Russian, and German literature and thought. This cosmopolitan background made the young girl take easily to internationalism. Lenin, too, used the term "internationalist" frequently. But, whereas she was to be active and a leader in the affairs of three parties, the Polish, the Russian, and the German, and in the International Congresses and Bureau, Lenin, wherever he lived, remained a Russian in exile, with gaze fixed on Russian affairs and Russian party squabbles.

Physically, the girl Rosa did not seem made to be a tragic heroine or a leader of men. A childhood hip ailment had left her body twisted, frail, and slight. She walked with an ungainly limp. But when she spoke, what people saw were large, expressive eyes glowing with compassion, sparkling with laughter, burning with combativeness, flashing with irony and scorn. When she took the floor at congresses or meetings, her slight frame seemed to grow taller and more commanding. Her voice was warm and vibrant (a good singing voice, too), her wit deadly, her arguments wide ranging and addressed, as a rule, more to the intelligence than to the feelings of her auditors.

She had been a precocious child, gifted with many talents. All her life, to the day of her murder in January, 1919, she was tempted and tormented by longings to diminish her absorption in politics in order to develop to the full the many other capacities of her spirit. Unlike so many political figures, her inner life, as expressed in her letters, her activities, her enthusiasms, reveals a rounded human being. She drew and painted, read great literature in Russian, Polish, German, and French, wrote poetry in the first three of these, continued to be seduced by an interest in anthropology, history, botany, geology, and others of the arts and sciences into which the modern specialized intellect is fragmented. "Interest" is but a cold word for the intensity with which she pursued her studies. A passage from one of her letters written from prison to the young friend of her last years, Dr. Hans Diefenbach, in the spring of 1917 will suffice to give an inkling of this passion:

> How glad I am that three years ago I suddenly threw myself into botanizing, as I do into all things, with all my ardor, with the whole of me, so that for me the world, the party, and the work vanished, and one single passion filled me day and night: to tramp about out there in the fields of spring, to fill my arms full of plants, then, back at home, to systematize them, put them in order, identify them, enter them in notebooks. How I lived in a fever all that Spring, how I suffered when I sat before some little plant and could not ascertain what it was and where it belonged! . . . In return for that now I am at home in the green world, I have conquered it for myself—in storm and passion —and whatever one seizes upon thus with ardor has firm roots in one.

It would not be amiss to suggest that this longing "to

conquer in storm and passion" was what made Rosa Luxemburg a "revolutionary" rather than a "reformist"
socialist.

Having been brought up in Russian Poland at a time
when its intellectuals were "discovering Marx," her initia-
tion into the revolutionary movement was precocious, too.
At sixteen, when she graduated at the top of her class
from the girls' gymnasium in Warsaw, she was denied the
gold medal because of "an oppositional attitude toward
the authorities." Three years later, at the tender age of
nineteen, she had to flee to Switzerland to avoid arrest,
aided both by a Catholic priest, who was given to understand that she was escaping from her parents to undergo
conversion, and by an underground Polish movement. (It
was the only time she fled arrest. Thereafter she was to
take prison terms as part of her work.)

At Zurich she made simultaneous entrance into the
world of refugee politics and the University. At the latter
she won two doctorates, one in law, the other in philosophy, acquiring at the same time her lifelong interest in a
half dozen other disciplines. Her doctoral thesis for the
law degree dealt with *The Industrial Development of
Poland*, economics then being under the Faculty of Juris-
prudence. Her thesis examined the close economic ties of
Russian Poland with the Russian market. She got to know
Plekhanov, Axelrod, Lenin, and other Russian exiles, and
three Polish exiles who worked with her thenceforward,
Marchlewski, Warszawski, and Jogiches.

Leo Jogiches,[1] three years older than Rosa, was, when
he fled to Zurich in 1890, already a fully formed conspirator and revolutionary. Almost immediately, they became
linked by a lifelong personal intimacy (without benefit of
religious or civil ceremony) and by a lifelong association

[1] Jogiches was also known as Lev Grozowski and Jan Tyszka, it being
common for men in the Polish and Russian underground to use a number
of aliases in their efforts to mystify the police. Sooner or later they were
likely to settle on one of these names because it had acquired prestige and
authority in their movement.

in the Polish and Russian, and later in the German, movements. The two were as different as two people engaged in a shared life and common enterprise could be. Jogiches was taciturn, stern, gloomy, secretive about his past and his private life, with none of her eloquence or outgoing capacity for friendship. Moreover, he was, as she was not, a consummate conspirator, an able organizer, a natural born faction fighter. Under the conditions of underground life in Poland and Russia, it is doubtful if she could have built a movement without him. She was the ideologist, he the organizer and conspirator. In Germany, however, where life was lived more publicly, he became a leader only by following in her wake. When they ceased to live together, his choice, not hers, he continued to be politically both her follower and mentor. As a foreigner, he could be active only in the Polish Social Democracy, until her murder caused him to risk his life in the Spartacus movement to avenge her and expose her murderers .

Switzerland was too small and peaceful, the political life of a Russian-Polish exile too confined, to give scope to her large talents and aspirations. She went for a while to France, where it is a measure of the breadth of her personal criteria that she was able to form friendships both with the outstanding Marxist leader, Vaillant, and with the great leader of the socialist "right," Jean Jaurès. "A splendid human being," she said of the latter, "open, natural, overflowing with inner warmth and intelligence." Her glowing temperament was closer to that of the humane, warmhearted Jaurès than to the more dogmatic Vaillant, the pedantic Kautsky, or the narrow, dictatorial Lenin.

The French movement, too, was too small to hold her, so she headed for Germany, the land where the "party of Marx and Engels" was the largest political party in the country and the largest and most influential in the international socialist movement. As a foreigner, she would find it impossible to become publicly active in Germany, so she proposed "marriage" to Gustav Luebeck, son of an old German socialist family she knew. After the wedding ceremony, the "couple" separated at the door of the marriage bureau, and "Frau Rosa Luebeck," a name she never used except to legitimatize her political activity, was free to plunge into the doctrinal and tactical disputes, the mass activities, the addressing of meetings and congresses, the writing for theoretical and popular journals. But not for that did she abandon her Polish and Russian activities, for this frail woman had enough overflowing spirits for three parties and nations.

Almost at the outset she rose to prominence in the great German party. She became a contributor to the theoretical organ, *Neue Zeit*, then assistant to its founder and editor, Karl Kautsky. She added her touch of fire and imagination to his doctrinaire fight against the "revision" of "orthodox" Marxism. She contributed to and became an editor of provincial dailies, then of the daily central organ, *Vorwaerts*. She got into the Vorstand (Executive), where even the veteran Bebel treated with respect her ardor, learning, wit, and sharp tongue. She became the teacher of Marxian economics at the Central Party Training School. Unlike other German pundits, who did little more than repeat Marx's formulae in "new" works, she developed first an original, mildly heretical interpretation of the labor theory of value (*Introduction to National Economy*) then ventured to cross swords with Marx himself in a critical appraisal and revision of the arid and weak Second Volume of *Das Kapital* (*The Accumulation of Capital*). Finally, from 1905 on, this redoubtable woman ("one of the last two remaining *men* in the German Social Democratic Party," she once said of herself to Bebel[2]) became a leader of an extreme left wing which considered even

[2] The "other man" was her friend and disciple, Clara Zetkin! Of Rosa Luxemburg, Clara Zetkin wrote that "strong self-mastery kept in leash the flaming glow of her being . . ."

the veterans of Marxist "orthodoxy," Kautsky and Bebel,
to be a mere "center" to her "left." Franz Mehring, the
biographer of Marx, called her "the most brilliant head
that has yet appeared among the scientific heirs of Marx
and Engels."

When Rosa Luxemburg was murdered by Prussian
officers in January, 1919, while being taken to prison, the
Leninists laid claim to her martyrdom, her tradition, and
her name. On the surface, this seemed a plausible claim.
For both Lenin and Luxemburg regarded themselves as
"revolutionary socialists." What they meant by this was
that they rejected root and branch the society in which
they lived, denied that it could be reformed or made better
in any meaningful fashion, insisted that it must be over-
thrown in a great upheaval and replaced by a totally new
society. One of Rosa Luxemburg's notable pamphlets,
Reform or Revolution (first published as two series of
articles in the *Leipziger Volkzeitung* in 1898 and 1899),
was an attempt to prove that modern industrial society,
the most rapidly changing in history, could not be fundamentally altered or improved except by a social revolution, and that such reforms as had been instituted were a
byproduct of the revolutionary movement rather than vol-
untary acts of society to remove abuses and redress griev-
ances. Legislation, constitutions, codified rights were but
the "vegetative stage of society"; its "creative stage" was
only and exclusively social revolution.

Both Lenin and Luxemburg were doctrinaire "lefts,"
too, in their low esteem for the activities of the organized
workingmen aiming at improving their conditions of life
within the framework of industrial (or, as they preferred
to say, "capitalist") society. Both denied the possibility of
any long term improvement. Both had a low opinion of
trade unions and of parliamentary activity. Neither could
ever understand why workingmen in general were not
more attracted to the historic "mission" which Marxism

had assigned them; why workers had no stomach for being reduced to "nought" the better to prepare themselves for becoming "all."[3] They never noticed nor understood that it was *against being reduced to nought* that the real workers' struggle was directed.

It was their common underestimation and misprision of the changes going on in industrial society, their common low opinion of reforms, and of trade union and parliamentary activities, that linked Lenin and Luxemburg together as "left" or "revolutionary" socialists. But here the resemblance between these two dissimilar temperaments ceases.

Their two names have also been linked by their opposition to the War of 1914-18. But Lenin, as we have seen, thought that a European war would be "a useful trick for the revolution" and "doubted that Nikolasha and Franz Josef will give us that pleasure." He welcomed war when it came, as "putting the bayonet on the order of the day," marking the longed for transition from the era of walking with "thin and weak soles on the civilized sidewalks of provincial cities" to the era that required "thick, hob-nailed boots" to climb the mountains. One of the "huge advantages" of any war, he said, was that it "mercilessly revealed, exposed and destroyed much that is rotten, outlived, moribund in human institutions."[4]

In contrast with his fierce exultation that bayonets were now on the order of the day, war came to Rosa Luxemburg as a burden of grief and anguish. The failure of the International to prevent it, or even decently to oppose it, above all the war-drunkenness of the ordinary socialist workers, plunged her into despair; for a time she seriously contemplated suicide. She sought to have the

[3] Cf. the lines of the socialist song, *The International:* "Arise ye slaves, no more in thrall, / The earth shall rise on new foundations, / We have been nought, we shall be all!"
[4] Lenin, *Collected Works*, 4th Russian Edition, Vol. XXI, pp. 184 and 222.

shattered International purify itself by merciless criticism of its errors, re-establish the broken ties of solidarity across the frontiers, sober up the war drunk masses, and unite them for a common struggle to bring about an early and a just peace by direct action.

"The slogan of peace," Lenin declared, "is stupid and wrong. . . . It signifies philistine moaning. . . ."

And again: "The slogan of peace is wrong—the slogan must be, turn the imperialist war into civil war." Luxemburg above all wanted to stop the war through mass action. Lenin wanted the war prolonged until the old order was in ruins, then prolonged further by its conversion into a universal civil war. Rosa Luxemburg was most concerned with the sufferings of the masses in war; Lenin with mobilizing their hatred. She wrote sadly of their chauvinistic madness; Lenin closed his eyes to, even denied, their chauvinism, picturing them as "betrayed by their leaders." She wished the International to be won back to its old pre-war position, restored and purified. He proposed that the International be split, and a Third or Communist International built on its ruins. When he used his control of Russia in 1918 to call a conference to found a new International, her movement sent a delegation instructed to oppose its formation. But at that moment, her murderers silenced her voice. She was an ardent fighter for her views but not by choice a splitter. Lenin's method had always been to fight for his views by splitting whatever he did not control.

Rosa Luxemburg wrote many pamphlets against Lenin's views and tactics, but no pamphlet in favor of them. Best known are her critique of his methods of organization and her critique of his dictatorship in Russia.

As soon as Lenin's views on centralism and dictatorship in his party became clear to her, she wrote in 1904 her anti-Leninist polemic entitled, *Organizational Questions of the Russian Social Democracy*. She published this as two articles simultaneously in Russian in *Iskra* and in

German in *Neue Zeit*. They were later republished as a pamphlet in those two languages, as well as in French and English under varying titles. In English it was published by the United Workers Party in the twenties, and then, in 1934, in a fresh translation by a man calling himself *Integer*, under the title *Revolutionary Socialist Organization*. Yet another version published in Glasgow by the Anti-Parliamentary Federation bore the title, *Leninism or Marxism?* The University of Michigan used the same title in publishing, in 1961, the present author's translation of two of Rosa Luxemburg's works against Lenin.

In two pamphlets and a number of articles published between 1902 and 1904, Lenin had been hammering away at his new organization plan for a "party of a new type," one differing fundamentally from all previous Marxian parties, whether founded by Marx and Engels in their own lifetime, or by their later disciples.

Reduced to its bare outlines, Lenin advanced the following propositions:

1. Left to its own devices and insights, the working class is incapable of developing any conception of the "historic mission" which Marx assigned to it. "The *spontaneous* development of the workers' movement leads precisely to its subordination to bourgeois ideology . . . the ideological enslavement of the workers to the bourgeoisie." (Lenin, Vol. V, pp. 355-56. Italics here and throughout as in the original.) What the workers' movement spontaneously concerns itself with is a "petty-bourgeois" matter, the price at which it sells the goods it possesses, namely its labor power. It wants but to get the best price and the best terms under the present "bourgeois" system. To do this it may fight the employers and even the state, but it will never develop the "socialist consciousness" necessary to its "historic mission."

2. Such "socialist consciousness"

can only be brought to the workers from the outside.

Alone, by their own forces, the working class is capable of developing a pure-and-simple trade union
consciousness. . . . But the teachings of socialism have
grown out of the philosophical, historical, economic
theories which were worked out by the educated representatives of the possessing classes. . . . (Vol. V,
pp. 347-48).

3. For this the working class needs a party which is
not made up of the working class but a party of guardians,
a self-constituted vanguard *for* the working class; an élite
party drawn from all classes, made up primarily of declassed
revolutionary intellectuals, who have made revolution their
profession. This party should lead and guide the working
class, inject its doctrine into the workers, infiltrate the
workingmen's organizations and struggles, and seek to use
them for its purposes. Only "bourgeois politicians," Lenin
wrote, "can believe that the task of a socialist is to serve
the workers in *their* struggles. The task of the socialist
politician is "not to assist the economic struggle of the proletariat, but to make the economic struggle assist the socialist movement and the victory of the revolutionary party."
(Vol. IV, p. 273.)

4. This classless élite, since it does the thinking for the
workingmen and seeks to inject its consciousness into them,
can appear even in countries where the working class is
backward and weak. It is an élite which is drawn from all
classes and must penetrate all classes (not only the working class), "dictating" to all classes; "dictating a positive
program of action, alike to rebellious students, to dissatis-
fied Zemstvo figures [i.e. leaders of the rural liberal nobility],
to discontented religious sectaries, to indignant school
teachers, etc." (Vol. V, p. 398). In short, it is to speak in
the name of the working class; it is to use that numerous
and closely packed class as its main battering ram in its
struggle for power, but is itself to supply the doctrine, the
watchwords, the purposes, the commands, the dictation.
It calls itself the "vanguard of the working class" because it

brings to, nay injects into, the working class its own consciousness of that class's "historic mission." But it is to be, no less, the overseer for the whole of society, the "dictator of the program" of all classes of society. In this bold, crude, repetitious hammering home of his ruthless doctrine, thus early can we discern the outlines of Lenin's future "dictatorship of the proletariat" over the proletariat and over society as a whole.

5. Such a "party of a new type" needs an organization of a new type. It should be organized like an army, have the unquestioning military discipline of an army, be centralized like an army, with all power and authority residing in its "general staff" or Central Committee. The Central Committee should plan, the local branches execute. The Central Committee should decide all general questions, the branches merely discuss how to grasp those decisions and carry them out. The Central Committee should have the right to form branches, dissolve them, purge them, appoint their leaders, eliminate, even exterminate the unworthy (Vol. V, p. 448; VI, pp. 211-15 and 221-23; VII, pp. 365-66).

The workers, schooled by life in factory and barracks, would take naturally to this. They have no time for "the toy forms of democracy." Bureaucracy and centralism in organization are truly revolutionary; democracy in party matters, however, is "opportunism in the organization question."

This last epithet shows that for his new dogmas Lenin was creating new transgressions, which required new names. Among them was *khvostism* (tailism, from Russian *khvost*, a tail), which meant that instead of directing, leading, pushing, and injecting your own purposes into the workers, you seek merely to serve them and their purposes, hence "drag at their tail." A kindred offense was "slavish kowtowing before spontaneity." (Vol. V, pp. 350-58.)

Rosa Luxemburg was offended in her whole being

by Lenin's worship of centralism, his implicit contempt for the working class, its own creative impulses and purposes, and his distrust of all spontaneous developments and spontaneity itself. It is here that her pamphlet joins issue with him.

Her polemical tone is, for her, remarkably gentle. She breaks a lance against his "pitiless ultra-centralism." She rightly pictures his future party as one in which the Central Committee will perpetuate itself, dictate to the party, and have the party dictate to the masses. The Central Committee would "be the only thinking element," the entire party and the masses being reduced to mere "executing limbs." She reminds him how many times in recent history the masses had shown "spontaneous creativeness," surprising the party, making a mockery of its pedantic formulae and recipes. With a marvellous sensitivity to what is in the air (this is 1904 and the storms of 1905 are approaching), she predicts that the masses will soon take the party leaders by surprise once more, again showing their own multiform creativeness and again overflowing the narrow channels of party prescription.

She closes with a plea for the autonomy of the masses, respect for their spontaneity and creativeness, respect also for their right to make their own mistakes and be helped by them. Her polemic ends with the words, so often quoted: "Let us speak plainly. Historically, the errors committed by a truly revolutionary movement are infinitely more fruitful than the infallibility of the cleverest Central Committee."

Nearly a quarter of a century passed. Lenin's party developed in the direction which Rosa Luxemburg had foreseen. In 1917, unexpectedly to all the socialist movements, the weak Tsar Nicholas II, having exhausted all social supports from Grand Dukes in his own family down, fell from power. For many months the real power was in the moods, whims, and will of millions of armed peasants in uniform, possessed by the idea of seizing the land, deserting the front, ending the war.

A provisional government arose, without any real apparatus of administration or enforcement, recognizing all the freedoms which Rosa believed in but holding that Russia was not "ripe" for socialism and that the cruel war must somehow be continued until Russia was safe from the invader and a general peace arrived at.

The real power remained "in the streets." By extreme appeals to demagogy, and by use of his tightly disciplined armed conspiracy calling itself a party, Lenin in November, 1917 was able to seize power "as easily as lifting up a feather" (Lenin, Vol. XXVII, p. 76).

From her prison cell, on the basis of oral accounts from visitors, scraps of news in German and Russian newspapers smuggled into her cell, Rosa began a short, friendly, yet necessarily critical, appraisal of what was happening in Russia. She intended it for publication as one of her underground *Spartacus Letters*. The "Letter," like its author, was to have a tragic history.

The little pamphlet was never altogether finished. On November 9, 1918, a democratic revolution in Germany opened the doors of Rosa Luxemburg's prison. She stepped out into a world she had not made and found herself "at the head" of a movement which looked to her for leadership but, being drunk with the heady wine of Lenin's success, could no longer comprehend her voice nor follow her lead. They had been so "Russified" that her differences with them were now of the same order, if not the same magnitude, as her differences with Lenin. Yet because they considered her their responsible leader she felt constrained to follow where they rushed.

In Germany elections were being held for a Constituent Assembly to write a new constitution for the new Germany. As a believer in democracy, she naturally assumed that her party (then calling itself *Spartakus* or the

Spartacans) would contest these universal, democratic elections. But Lenin in Russia had dispersed by force of arms a democratically elected Constituent Assembly, proclaiming instead a "Government of the Workers' and Soldiers' Councils"—in actual fact, a government of his party. Rosa's "followers" outvoted her, deciding to boycott the elections to the German Constituent Assembly and proclaim a "Government of the Workers' and Soldiers' Councils" of Germany. Her party dragged its reluctant leaders in its wake.

A week after her release from prison, in the first issue of their new paper, *Rote Fahne* (dated Nov. 18, 1918), she made a solemn pledge to the masses:

> The Spartacus League will never take over governmental power in any other way than through the clear, unambiguous will of the great majority of the proletarian masses in all Germany, never except by virtue of their conscious assent to the views, aims, and fighting methods of the Spartacus League.

But in the third week of December, the masses, as represented in the First National Congress of the Councils of Workers' and Soldiers' Deputies, rejected by an overwhelming majority the Spartacan motion that the Councils should disrupt the Constituent Assembly and the Provisional Democratic Government and seize power themselves.

In the light of Rosa's public pledge, the duty of her movement seemed clear: to accept the decision, or to seek to have it reversed not by force but by persuasion. However, on the last two days of 1918 and the first of 1919, the Spartacans held a convention of their own where they outvoted their "leader" once more. In vain did she try to convince them that to oppose both the Councils and the Constituent Assembly with their tiny forces was madness and a breaking of their democratic faith. They voted to try to take power in the streets, that is by armed

uprising. Almost alone in her party, Rosa Luxemburg
decided with a heavy heart to lend her energy and her
name to their effort.

The *Putsch,* wth inadequate forces and overwhelming mass disapproval except in Berlin, was as she had
predicted, a fizzle. But neither she nor her close associates
fled for safety as Lenin had done in July, 1917. They
stayed in the capital, hiding carelessly in easily suspected
hideouts, trying to direct an orderly retreat. On January
16, a little over two months after she had been released
from prison, Rosa Luxemburg was seized, along with Karl
Liebknecht and Wilhelm Pieck. Reactionary officers murdered Liebknecht and Luxemburg while "taking them to
prison." Pieck was spared, to become, as the reader knows,
one of the puppet rulers of Moscow-controlled East Germany.

Leo Jogiches spent the next few days exposing the
murderers, until his arrest. He was taken to the Moabit
Prison, where Radek, Lenin's emissary to the Spartacans
and to any German forces which the Russian ruler "might
do business with," was also taken. On March 10, Jogiches
was dragged out and murdered, but Radek, armored by
investiture with a fragment of Lenin's governmental power,
was permitted to sit in his cell, holding court for German
officers and German heavy industrialists as well as German
communists, and beginning the negotiations which led to
the Reichswehr-Red Army secret military agreement, fore-
shadow of the future Stalin-Hitler Pact. In its way, the
fate of the Russian emissary Radek and the "Russified"
Pieck on the one hand, and that of Rosa Luxemburg on
the other, are fitting symbols of the differences between
Luxemburg's and Lenin's conceptions of the relationship
between socialist principles and power.[5] To Radek Rosa

[5] For an account of the secret agreement initiated by Radek and Von
Seeckt, see Hilger and Meyer, *The Incompatible Allies,* New York, 1953;
Kochan, *Russia and the Weimar Republic,* Cambridge, England, 1954;
Gerald Freund, *Unholy Alliance,* New York, 1957; Hans W. Gatzke,
"Russo-German Military Collaboration During the Weimar Republic," in
The American Historical Review, April, 1958, pp. 565-597.

Luxemburg had said in November 1918, "Terror has not crushed us. How can you put your trust in terror?"

Rosa Luxemburg's little treatise on the Russian Revolution continued to have a pathetic career. The growing subordination of the Spartacan Movement, germ of the future Communist Party, to Lenin and Russian communism, caused her friends to suppress her work. They said that she had "lacked adequate information," that it was "untimely" to publish it (it is still "untimely" for them today!), nor did they scruple to say that she had "changed her mind" on her views of a lifetime as expressed in it.

When the censorship by her own comrades was at last broken, it was by one of her closest associates, Paul Levi. But he published the pamphlet only when he was breaking with Lenin and Leninism out of disgust with another attempted *Putsch* and with Lenin himself, who secretly agreed with him but for reasons of political expediency publicly excoriated him for his open criticism of his party's errors. Zealous young communists were told that he was violating Rosa Luxemburg's cherished wish to have it suppressed, and that they would read it only at their souls' peril. The Social Democrats took it up, both in Germany and in France, where it was published in *Le Populaire* in 1922, but the communists read only distorting commentaries and refutations. The unfortunate little classic was made a faction football and kicked around until it disappeared from view.

The disease which Rosa had foreseen as inseparable from a Russian- and Lenin-dominated International did indeed infect the Comintern. As its "Stalinization" in the middle and late twenties extruded one group after another of the original founders, the communist "splinter groups" thus arising felt the need of understanding the process of the decay of the Communist International from a supposed international association of brother parties into an agency of the Russian State, Party, and Dictator. Both Rosa's 1904 articles on the Leninist organization plan and

her critical appraisal of the Russian Revolution were revived once more.

All around her, the Russian Revolution was regarded
with blind hatred or blind idolatry. But in the darkness
of her prison cell, in a land made doubly dark by war and
by her movement's betrayal of its anti-war pledges, she
did not let the light she thought she descried in the Eastern
sky blind her to the dangers inherent in Lenin's method
of seizing and using power.

The great service of the Bolsheviks, she thought, was
to have "put socialism on the order of the day," to have
begun to feel for a way out of the shambles of war, to
have redeemed the tarnished honor of international socialism. But this was no model revolution carried on under
model laboratory conditions. It had occurred in the midst
of war and alien invasion, in a backward land, cursed with
poverty, lacking in a democratic tradition, ill-equipped
economically and culturally for the building of a "higher"
social order. "It would be a crazy idea to think that every
last thing done and left undone under such abnormal conditions should represent the very pinnacle of perfection. . . ."

The heart of her pamphlet, as of her activities and
teachings, lay in her unshakeable belief in the initiative
and capacity of the mass of mankind. That had been the
real principle of her disagreement with Lenin in 1904 as
it was now, two months before her death. To her the
health-giving force of socialism was an attempt to extend
democracy still further, to strengthen the pulse-beat of
public life, to awaken hitherto inert masses to activity, to
awareness of their own capacities for achievement and
correction of their own errors, to initiative for the direct,
popular solution of all problems, to the assumption of control over "their own" party, "their own" state machine,
over industry, and over their own destinies. Her strategy

rested upon her belief that the masses were instinctively and universally revolutionary. She was certain that they needed only to be enlightened as to their true interests. So strong was her own revolutionary urge and so logical her dialectical explanation of the imminence of capitalist collapse that they obscured from her the fact that the masses, like their leaders, were caught up by the current of their age.

There were more contradictory elements in her broad view than in Lenin's narrow authoritarian conception, for she knew too much of revolutions and was too much a revolutionary to reject the employment of a temporary dictatorship to defend the "new order" from overthrow by its still existent enemies. But she regarded such dictatorship as an evil, even if under some circumstances a necessary one, an evil to be mitigated as much as possible by making it as temporary as possible and limiting its scope as far as possible, while offsetting its dictatorial potential by greatly extending its exact opposite and antidote, freedom. The one hope of preventing a degeneration of a revolution even in its victory lay to her mind in the simultaneous overall extension of democracy and freedom to the widest possible number of human beings.

> Freedom only for the supporters of the government, only for the members of one party—however numerous they may be—is no freedom at all. Freedom is always and exclusively freedom for the one who thinks differently. Not because of any fanatical concept of "justice" but because all that is instructive, wholesome, and purifying in political freedom depends on this essential characteristic, and its effectiveness vanishes when "freedom" becomes a special privilege.

Is there any regime which loves liberty which could not be proud to engrave these three sentences over the portals of its public buildings?

As a socialist, she wanted socialism introduced, but she knew that her ideal of socialism could not be intro-

duced without the widest possible democracy and freedom.
No party, she felt, had a monopoly of wisdom, or a filing
cabinet full of ready-made solutions to the thousands of
new problems that would present themselves in the course
of carrying on an "old order" and still more in the course
of trying to institute a "new." The actual solutions were to
her neither a matter of authority nor prescription but of
endless experiment, of fruitful trial and error, and fruitful
correction of error.

> Socialism by its very nature cannot be introduced by
> *ukase.* . . . Only unobstructed, effervescing life falls
> into a thousand new forms and improvisations, brings
> to light creative force, itself corrects all mistaken at-
> tempts.

Her "worship of spontaneity," her rejection of authori-
tarianism, were further apart from Lenin's views than ever.
The differences of 1904 had grown as the occasion for their
expression had grown. How prophetic do her words sound
now, a half century after they were written:

> With the repression of political life in the land as a
> whole, life in the Soviets must also become more and
> more crippled. Without general elections, without
> unrestricted freedom of press and assembly, without
> a free struggle of opinions, life dies out in every
> public institution, becomes a mere semblance of life,
> in which only the bureaucracy remains the active ele-
> ment. Public life gradually falls asleep, a few dozen
> party leaders of inexhaustible energy and boundless
> experience direct and rule. Among them, in reality,
> only a dozen outstanding heads do the leading and an
> elite of the working class is invited from time to time
> to meetings where they are to applaud the speeches
> of the leaders, and to approve proposed resolutions
> unanimously—at bottom then, a clique affair—a dic-
> tatorship to be sure, not however of the proletariat
> but only of a handful of politicians. . . . Such conditions

must inevitably cause a brutalization of public life: attempted assassinations, shooting of hostages, etc.

Much of what Rosa Luxemburg wrote in this little pamphlet is now hopelessly dated, for much of it stems from dogmas which would not bear examination and have not resisted the passage of time. Yet how much of the half century of subsequent Soviet development did she foresee in the darkness of her prison cell! How alive is her love of liberty, and her astonishing ability to put into memorable words that love of freedom! It is these qualities, along with her astonishing powers of foresight of where ruthless dictatorship would lead, that make her six-decade-old, unfinished pamphlet of more than merely biographical and historical interest. It is, as it has come to be widely recognized, a classic of that now vanished Marxian socialist movement in which she was so ardent a crusader.

7

Inessa Armand

IN MARCH, 1963, I published an article in the *Slavic Review* titled "Lenin and Inessa Armand." In February, 1964, the same article was published in the British magazine, *Encounter*. In both cases, Moscow took no notice. But when *Time* made reference to it in their issue of April 24, 1964, with a cover drawing of Lenin by Ben Shahn, the Moscow authorities closed the *Time* bureau and expelled its correspondent. *Time*, said *Izvestia* by way of explanation, had "smeared what was dear and sacred to every Soviet person" and "touched with dirty fingers the memory of the founder of the Soviet State." At the same time, a spate of somewhat inaccurate and trivial articles about the almost forgotten Inessa Armand filled the Soviet press on what would have been her ninetieth birthday had she lived, and her daughter, "little Inessa," was the subject of a special childhood profile in *Pravda*. Here is the story of Lenin and Inessa Armand as I reconstructed it, primarily from Soviet sources.[1] From it the reader can judge who has touched her memory or Lenin's with "dirty fingers."

[1] See Appendix page 164.

In 1924, immediately after Lenin died, the Central Committee of his party called upon all who had a shred of writing from his hand to deposit it in the party's archives. The holders hastened to comply. All his letters were ostensibly published in three substantial volumes, supplemented by items in a number of "Miscellany" (*Sbornik*) volumes. Not one letter to or from Inessa Armand appeared in that flood of Leniniana.

On February 27, 1939, Lenin's wife, Krupskaya, died. Four months after her death, *Bolshevik* (No. 13, July, 1939) published the first of two letters from Lenin to Inessa on the "woman question." The letters were not so much an expression of Lenin's views as a comment on Inessa Armand's. Planning in the course of her Bolshevik work with "working women" to write a brochure addressed to them, Inessa had dutifully submitted her outline to Lenin. Among her programmatic demands for woman's rights she included "free love." The Marx-Lenin Institute has not chosen to publish any of her letters to Lenin, although from a French communist, Jean Fréville, who was permitted to consult her letters to Lenin when writing an authorized biography of Inessa, we know that the Institute has them. Something of the nature of her plan, however, we can glean from Lenin's letter concerning it, in which he quotes hers. But first we must consider his letters to Inessa Armand as a whole.[2]

The first thing that strikes the Russian reader of Lenin's letters to Inessa is the use of the intimate pronoun *ty* in addressing her, in place of the usual polite second person pronoun *vy*. To the English-speaking reader it is hard to convey how unusual, and how intimate, it is for an educated Russian to address a woman as *ty*. Or for that matter to address another man thus, unless they were childhood intimates, companions from youth, members of

[2] In 1952, twenty-four of his letters to her—manifestly somewhat cut and usually deprived of their salutation and complimentary closing—were published in Vol. XXXV of Lenin's *Works*.

the same family, or much closer to each other than adult friends and socialist comrades. In all the 600-odd published letters of Lenin, except for his mother, his two sisters, and his wife, Inessa is the only woman to whom he ever wrote *ty*. Only two men ever received a letter with the intimate personal address. Both were comrades of his youth, one being Martov, for whom, as Krupskaya testifies in her *Memories of Lenin,* he felt a lifelong attachment.[3] Yet there is only one letter extant in which he wrote *ty* to Martov. After their first political disagreement he never again addressed him except as *vy*.[4] The other was Krzhizhanovsky, who in the nineties lived near him as a fellow exile in distant Siberia along the Yenisei, for weeks on end sharing with him the same cabin. With Krzhizhanovsky, too, after the latter crossed him once in politics, though he afterwards returned to unquestioning discipleship, Lenin never again used anything but *vy*.[5]

Neither Krassin, who made Lenin's bombs in 1905 and became his Commissar of Trade in 1918, nor Bogdanov, who was his chief lieutenant after the break with *Iskra,* nor Zinoviev, who held the same place from 1908 to 1917, nor Bukharin, whom he called the "darling of the party," nor Sverdlov nor Stalin, who each in turn became his chief organization man, ever received a letter that used the intimate pronoun. Sparing as most educated Russians are in the use of *ty* with each other, Lenin was even more so than most, always maintaining a subtle distance between himself and the closest and most useful of his dis-

[3] This is testified to by every mention of Martov in the two volumes of Krupskaya's *Vospominaniya* and by M. Gorky, *V. I. Lenin* (Moscow, 1931), p. 43. Krupskaya relates that when Lenin felt his end was near, one of his last utterances was a mournful query: "They say that Martov is dying, too!"

[4] Lenin, XXXIV, 117-18 (the *ty* letter), and p. 146 (the first *vy* letter). Between the two letters, seven months apart, had come the fateful disagreement on the definition of a member and on the composition of the *Iskra* editorial board.

[5] Lenin, XXXIV, 113-14, 127, 186-88; XXXV, 370-71, 375-76, 397, 399, 400, 405, 406-7, 409-10, 414, 415, 422, 423-34, 431, 456, 472. All the letters in Vol. XXXV use *vy*.

ciples. Nor, to mention the women who served him longest and most faithfully and for whose work he was most grateful, did he ever write *ty* to Stasova, Ludmila Stal, Lilina Zinoviev, Alexandra Kollontay, or Angelica Balabanoff. Any of them would have been astonished had he done so.

In the letters to Inessa Armand, too, there is a sudden change from *ty* to *vy*, but not out of cooling friendship or disagreement. In his first published letter to Inessa Armand Lenin uses the intimate form, and he continues to do so until the day war is declared. Then, with wartime censors opening letters on every frontier, he drops the telltale *ty* for the more formal *vy*, for Lenin was conspiratorial even in this. Otherwise there is no change in tone.[6]

Inessa Armand was a dedicated, romantic heroine, who seemed to come out of the pages of Chernyshevsky's *What Is To Be Done?*—Lenin's favorite revolutionary novel as it was Inessa's. Indeed, Chernyshevsky's novel was the chief instrument of the conversion of Inessa to socialism. The true story of her life has been obscured by the accounts of those who did not know her intimately, and by an understandable reticence on the part of those who did. The sketch of her in the *Bolshaya Sovetskaya Entsiklopediia* is meager, omits what is most important in her career, and is mistaken even as to the date of her birth and true name.

The Encyclopedia gives her birth date as 1875, her name as Inessa Fedorovna (i.e., Inessa, daughter of Fedor), and her maiden name as Stephanie. Actually, she was born in Paris in 1874, of a French father and a Scot-

---

[6] The last letter using *ty* is dated July 15, 1914. The first wartime letter is dated by the Marx-Lenin Institute as "written in September 1914." One cannot tell whether Lenin thinks of her as *ty* or *vy* because, for the first time in his life, Lenin tries to write the whole letter, except two impersonal sentences, in English. It remained unpublished until 1960, when a Russian translation (with no original) was published in *Voprosy Istorii KPSS*, No. 4, 1960, pp. 3-4. Then there were no letters until the war was five months old because Inessa joined Lenin and Krupskaya in Berne as soon as they got to Switzerland. But when they separated and there was occasion to write her once more, on January 17, 1915, Lenin wrote *vy*.

tish mother, both music hall artists, and was christened
Elizabeth d'Herbenville. The Inessa by which she came
exclusively to be known was the name she assumed in
Russia for party work. So much did she become known
by it (though she sometimes used the pseudonym Blo-
nina instead) that when she died, the obituary written
by Krupskaya for *Pravda* was headed with the single
word: "Inessa." The maiden name Stephanie given her
in the Encyclopedia is an obvious misunderstanding of
her father's stage name, for in the French theater he was
billed as Stéphen. The name Petrova or Petrovna, given
by some sources, is the pseudonym she used when she
appeared in Brussels on Lenin's behalf in July, 1914, to
defy the International Socialist Bureau, which was trying
to unify the Russian socialist movement. It was as Comrade Petrova that she delivered in French the speech
Lenin had written for her; it was as Petrova that the police
agent present reported on her. It was an appropriate name,
for it is derived from *petra*, "rock," and signifies that she,
as a good Leninist, was "rock hard" and would stand up
against all the great men of the International, firm as a
rock.

Her childhood was that of a daughter of people of
the theater. Her father, Pécheux d'Herbenville, was a
comedian and singer, known on the stage as Stéphen. Her
mother sang in French and gave singing and piano lessons. As a child Inessa learned to speak both her native
French and her mother's English tongue with equal flu-
ency. The world of music and the stage were her home.
When her father died and her mother could no longer
support three fatherless children by teaching or music
hall work, the girl, Elizabeth, was taken to Russia by a
French aunt and her English maternal grandmother, both
of whom secured positions, as was the fashion of the day,
tutoring in French and English respectively the children of
a wealthy Russian industrialist of French descent, Evgenii
Armand, a textile manufacturer in Pushkino, thirty miles

from Moscow. Here the young girl grew up in a family with liberal views. She was accepted on an equal footing with the children of the Armand family.

At fourteen she too was provided with a tutor, who turned out to be a man of advanced, perhaps revolutionary, ideas. These she did not understand, but they excited her imagination. She mastered Russian, was introduced into the Orthodox Church, and shared the interests that prevailed in educated circles in the closing years of nineteenth-century Russia. By now she spoke faultless German and Russian as well as French and English—polyglot talents that would make her invaluable to Lenin. Her aunt, who had been a teacher of singing and piano, taught her to be a virtuoso at the piano, another talent that Lenin was to prize. At eighteen she married Alexander Evgenevich Armand, the manufacturer's second son, slightly older than she. The couple moved to the nearby estate of the Armands at Eldigino, and later to Moscow. She lived with her husband for many quiet, apparently happy years, bearing him five children, three boys and two girls. But this substantial family, in the words of Krupskaya's memoir, "did not prevent her from going her own path all the same, and becoming a revolutionary Bolshevik."[7]

It was her husand's older brother, Boris Evgenevich, who by word and example first steered her course towards "advanced ideas." He took the side of the workingmen in his father's factory, tried to organize them, and was questioned by the police when they traced to him the ownership of a mimeograph machine on which his unsigned leaflets were being reproduced. It was most likely he who put into his sister-in-law's hands Chernyshevsky's novel, *Chto delat'?*, on whose utopian heroes and heroine, Vera Pavlovna, Inessa sought to model her own life.[8]

[7] "Inessa," by N. Krupskaya, in *Pravda*, Oct. 3, 1920.
novel, which took the Russian intelligentsia by storm with its image of the "new men," also contained a "new woman," its heroine, Vera
[8] A common bond between Lenin and Inessa Armand on their first meeting was their shared admiration for Chernyshevsky's novel. This

Like so many idealistic women of her generation,
Inessa was not content with the sheltered career of wife
and mother. Like her heroine, she too wanted to be "socially useful," to help the less fortunate members of her
sex. She tried running the farm on her husband's estate,
then teaching and doing works of charity. In time, the
problem of prostitution became her obsession. She sought
to redeem these unhappy women from their life of deg-
radation, but was shocked to find them suspicious, un-
ashamed, unwilling to be "redeemed." Since one of her
sources of inspiration was Leo Tolstoy, she went to this
fountainhead of wisdom for counsel. His answer ("Nothing will come of your work. It was so before Moses, it was
so after Moses. So it was, so it will be")[9] turned her away
from Tolstoyanism to a more exclusive dedication to Chernyshevsky. She would imitate Vera Pavlovna and her "uncommon" friends and tutors in their efforts to transform
the structure of society. Thus she would put an end, she
thought, to the hateful institution which had existed be-

Pavlovna. The American anarchist Benjamin Tucker, who translated it into
English, wrote of the novel: "The fundamental idea is that woman is a
human being and not an animal created for man's benefit, and its chief
purpose is to show the superiority of free unions between men and women
over the indissoluble marriage sanctioned by the Church and State." Preface to the fourth edition (New York, 1909), p. 3.
   If Lenin was attracted by the vision of the "uncommon men" and
their "rigorist" leader concerning utopia, Inessa was attracted by the deeds
and views of the novel's heroine. In the work entitled *In Memory of Inessa
Armand* Krupskaya wrote: "Inessa was moved to socialism by the image
of woman's rights and freedom in *What Is To Be Done?*" Like the heroine,
she broke her ties with one man to live with another, concerned herself
with good deeds to redeem the poor female and the prostitute, tried to
solve the problems of woman's too servile place in society. Indeed, whole
generations of Russian radicals were influenced by Chernyshevsky's many-
sided utopian novel and were moved to imitate its "uncommon men and
women." Just as Marx could be the spiritual ancestor of people as various as Bernstein, Kautsky, Bebel, and Luxemburg, so Chernyshevsky was
a formative influence for the two men who in their persons incarnated the
two opposing poles of socialism in 1917: Tsereteli and Lenin. If Inessa
found in the novel her image of woman's rights and freedom in love, and
Lenin the prototypes of his vanguard and his leadership, Tsereteli found
there his ideal of service to the people. Men who are big enough to have
spiritual progeny are likely to be thus many-sided and complicated, while
each "descendant" finds in his "ancestor" that which enlarges and reinforces
what already exists in him.
   [9] *In Memory of Inessa Armand*, p. 7.

fore Moses and which neither the Laws given to Moses nor the coming of Christ had been able to change. It was with "the woman problem in its relation to socialism" that she concerned herself for the rest of her life. She left husband and children, apparently without bitter scenes or rancor (just as Vera Pavlovna left Lopukhov). Later she sent for her two youngest to live with her abroad. But unlike her model, who was eager to earn her own way, Inessa continued to receive support from her husband all her life— until Lenin's seizure of power put an end to the fortune of the Armands in Russia.

In 1904 at the age of thirty, Inessa made her final break with her husband (they sometimes met as friends as occasion permitted thereafter), and went to Sweden to study feminism at the feet of Ellen Key. In Stockholm's Russian colony she got to know of Lenin's *What's to be Done?*, a title that reverberated in her spirit. In his organizational principles, his doctrine of the elite or vanguard, his hard line, she must have felt an echo of Rakhmetov, the "rigorist" of Chernyshevsky's novel. Thus before she met Lenin, she became his admirer and a Leninist.

An organizing mission for the Bolsheviks sent her back to Russia, where she landed almost immediately in prison, on January 6, 1905. The October Manifesto of the Tsar, promising freedom and a constitution, contained an amnesty provision for politicals which released her. On April 9, 1907, she was arrested a second time for Bolshevik activities in the armed forces. Her husband furnished bail, but she landed in jail once more while awaiting trial, and from jail was deported by administrative order to Archangel Province in Russia's far north for a two-year period. She managed to flee abroad before her term was quite over.

Early in 1910 she went to Paris where she got to know the Ulyanovs. Lenin, Zinoviev, and Kamenev (then the *troika*) had just moved to Paris in December, 1909. The leading Menshevik exiles were there too, and many Socialist

Revolutionaries, so that Paris possessed a big Russian colony, in which Inessa soon assumed a leading position. She came with two of her children, a boy, André, and a girl, Ina. "She was a very ardent Bolshevik," writes Krupskaya, "and soon gathered our Paris crowd around her."

Those who knew her then remember her somewhat strange, nervous, slightly asymmetrical face, unruly, dark chestnut hair, great hypnotic eyes, and inextinguishable ardor of spirit. She had a wider culture than any other woman in Lenin's circle (at least until Kollontay became an adherent of his during the war), a deep love of music, above all of Beethoven, who became Lenin's favorite too. She played the piano like a virtuoso, was fluent in five languages, was enormously serious about Bolshevism and work among women, and possessed personal charm and an intense love of life to which almost all who wrote of her testify.[10] When Lenin met her, she had just turned thirty-six.

In the course of his factional war with the Vperyodist Bolsheviks,[11] who had set up a party school in Gorky's home in Capri, Lenin rejected their invitation to teach, promoted (unwittingly aided by a police agent) a split in their student body, and opened a rival school in Longjumeau, near Paris. Inessa rented a large building there and set up lodgings and a dining room for the students. The Ulyanovs dined there too. As a rare mark of Lenin's confidence, she was permitted to alternate with him in the course on political economy. The rest of the faculty were

[10] The one exception is Angelica Balabanoff, who got to know her five years later through their joint work in the Zimmerwald and Kienthal wartime conferences, and the International Woman's and Youth's meetings. Dr. Balabanoff told me: "I did not warm to Inessa. She was pedantic, a one hundred per cent Bolshevik in the way she dressed (always in the same severe style), in the way she thought, and spoke. She spoke a number of languages fluently, and in all of them repeated Lenin verbatim."

[11] For this controversy, see my *Three Who Made a Revolution*, Chapter 29.

Zinoviev and Kamenev. No other Bolshevik woman had
ever been so honored.

The Ulyanovs generally held everyone at arm's length,
with Krupskaya as self-appointed guardian to see that
Lenin's work and privacy were not interfered with. But by
1911 it had become obvious to the little circle of Russian
émigrés that Inessa had somehow breached the barrier:
"He was often seen with her at a café on the Avenue
d'Orleans. . . . It struck even so unobservant a person as
the French Socialist-Bolshevik, Charles Rappaport. Lenin,
he wrote, "avec ses petits yeux mongols épiait toujours
cette petite française. . . ."[12]

The Ulyanovs now moved to 4, Rue Marie-Rose, and
Inessa and her children to Number 2 of the same street.
(The houses are still standing, in good condition, with a
plaque outside Number 4 telling the passerby that Lenin
once lived there.) "The house grew brighter when Inessa
entered it," Krupskaya was to write six years after Inessa's
death.[13]

In 1912 Lenin completed the final split in the Social
Democratic Party by designating his Bolshevik conference
in Prague an official party congress, and declaring Martov,
Axelrod, Plekhanov, Trotsky, and their followers "outside
the party" until they submitted to his "Congress." He
moved to Krakow, in Austrian Poland, to be nearer St.
Petersburg, where the legal daily *Pravda* now began to
appear. To line up the underground inside Russia, he sent
Inessa, who had also moved to Krakow, on a clandestine
tour of Russia. There were so many police agents in his
underground now that almost immediately she landed in

[12] Valentinov, *op. cit.*, p. 99.
[13] The quotations from Krupskaya, here and throughout the article,
are either from her account in *In Memory of Inessa Armand* or from Vol.
II of her *Memories of Lenin*. In the English-language edition, *Memories of
Lenin* (New York: International Publishers, 1930), they are quoted from
pp. 58, 66, 67, 73, 84, 90, 121, 123, 124, 125, 126, 128, 130, and 150.
Where the translation seemed poor, I have retranslated from the corres-
ponding pages of the 1957 Russian edition.

prison once more. When she developed signs of tuberculosis in jail, her husband managed to get her out on bail after a year in prison. She immediately rejoined Lenin and his wife in Krakow and in Poronin in the Tatra Mountains.

> We were terribly glad . . . at her arrival. . . . In the autumn [of 1913] all of us became very close to Inessa. In her there was much joy of life and ardor. We had known Inessa in Paris, but there was a large colony there. In Krakow lived a small closely knit circle of comrades. Inessa rented a room in the same family with which Kamenev lived.[14]

> My mother became closely attached to Inessa. Inessa often went to talk with her, sit with her, have a smoke with her. It became cosier and gayer when Inessa came. Our entire life was filled with party concerns and affairs, more like a student commune than like family life, and we were glad to have Inessa. . . . Something warm radiated from her talk.

> Ilyich, Inessa, and I often went on walks together. Zinoviev and Kamenev dubbed us the "hikers" party. We walked in the meadows on the outskirts of the city. Meadow in Polish is *blon,* and Inessa from then on took the pseudonym of *Blonina.* Inessa was a good musician, urged us all to go to Beethoven concerts, and played very well many of Beethoven's pieces. Ilyich especially loved *Sonate Pathétique,* constantly begging her to play it.

In 1921, when Lenin had taken power and Inessa was dead, one day he said to Gorky:

> I know nothing that is greater than the *Appassionata:* I am ready to listen to it every day. It is amazing, more than human, music. I want to say gentle stupidities and stroke the heads of people who, living in this dirty hell, can create such beauty. But today you must not stroke the head of anyone—they will bite your hand.

[14] The Kamenevs lived on an upper floor in the same building as the Ulyanovs.

It is necessary to beat them over the head, beat without
mercy, even though in our ideal we are against the use
of force against people. Hm-hm, duty is hellishly
hard![15]

It was this side of Lenin's nature—the side which he
strove mightily, and on the whole successfully, to restrain
—that Inessa ministered to. The gentleness she evoked in
him (the desire to say gentle stupidities and stroke the
heads of people) is reflected in his letters to her, despite
the censorship to which they have been subjected, reflected
even in letters arguing with her when she has disagreed
and pressed her point hard.[15]

Life in Krakow proved too cramping for Inessa's overflowing energies. She made a tour of the Bolshevik exile
colonies, lecturing on the woman question, and then returned to her native Paris, where the main Bolshevik group
abroad was settled.

At the beginning of January, 1914, Lenin stopped over
in Paris with Duma Deputy (and police agent) Malinovsky, when they were on their way to address a Lettish
Congress in Brussels. He returned to Paris alone, spending
a month and a half in the French capital. To his mother he
wrote on February 21: "I have just been in Paris, not a
bad trip. Paris is not a good city to live in with modest
means, and quite an exhausting one. But to be there a
little while, to visit, to wander about a bit—there's not a
better nor a gayer city. It refreshed me greatly."[16]

No letter of Lenin's ever suggested a happier, more
relaxed mood.

It was while Inessa was living in Paris and the Ulyanovs were in Krakow, that Lenin's first letter to her was
written. The published version has been censored and lacks

[15] *Lenin i Gorkii: Pisma* . . . , (Moscow, 1958), pp. 251-52. An English translation is in Maxim Gorky, *Days with Lenin* (New York, 1932), p.
52.
[16] Lenin, XXXVII, 430.

salutation and closing and all personal touches. His last
letter to her is dated in his works as "written between the
25th and the 31st of March, 1917," that is, after the February Revolution had begun, and both Inessa and Lenin
were getting ready to go to Russia. She was one of the
eighteen Bolsheviks who accompanied him across Germany
to Russia in the "sealed train" that enabled them to reach
Petrograd on April 16, 1917.

During the war Lenin wrote more letters to Inessa
Armand than to any other person, whether relative or
disciple. As soon as he got out of prison in Austria and
reached a safe haven in Berne, Switzerland, he wrote to
Inessa, who because of her lung ailment was living in the
Swiss Alps at Les Avants. Except for the first two sentences,
Lenin writes this time as best he can in English. He tells
Inessa of the need to gather materials on the war positions
of all parties, then asks about her health, whether she eats
better, whether she has books and newspapers, how the
weather is in Les Avants, whether she is taking walks, and
whether they can see each other soon. The letter must
have been written after September 6. "Towards the middle
of September," according to her official biographer, Inessa
moved to Berne.[17] Thereafter there were no letters to
Inessa for the rest of the autumn. A passage in Krupskaya's
memoirs explains why:

> The memory of that autumn is interwoven in my mind
> with the autumnal scene in the forest in Berne. The
> autumn of that year was a glorious one. We lived in
> Berne on a small, neat, quiet street bordering on the
> Berne Forest. . . . Cater-corner across the road lived
> Inessa [the street was Distelweg]. . . . We would
> wander for hours along the forest roads covered with
> fallen yellow leaves. Generally the three of us went
> together on these walks, Vladimir Ilyich, Inessa, and I.
> Sometimes we would sit for hours on the sunlit, wooded
> mountainside, while Ilyich jotted down outlines of his

[17] Fréville, *Inessa Armand,* p. 90.

speeches and articles . . . I would study Italian . . .
Inessa would sew a skirt and bask with delight in the
autumnal sun. . . .

As soon as Inessa left Berne, Lenin resumed writing to
her. In the brief period from November 20, 1916, to the
outbreak of the February Revolution in 1917, he wrote
fourteen letters to her, two brief notes to his younger sister,
one to his older sister's husband, and four to other persons
—in short, more to her than to all the rest put together. In
his letters to Inessa, as always, preoccupation with politics
is uppermost. But tone and depth reveal facets of his
nature exhibited in no other letters, whether to members
of his family or to other disciples.

Unlike the letters to other intimates of the Ulyanovs,
there are in the letters to Inessa no mention of Krupskaya,
no regards from her, nor any personal note added by her.
Only after Lenin has been writing to Inessa for three years
does he once mention Krupskaya: "Nadia is ill: she caught
bronchitis and has a fever. It seems she will have to toss
about in bed for a while. Today I called a woman doctor."[18]

Several letters sound a rare note akin to self-pity and
search for sympathy: how hard his life is, how unending
and ungrateful his factional struggles, how dumb even the
best Bolsheviks can be. Thus in the earliest letter from
Krakow to Paris in December, 1913, he tells her that he is
receiving protests from offended party cells because he does
not work through them but picks his own men of confidence for confidential tasks:

> Clowns! They chase after words. Don't think how
> devilishly complicated and tricky life is which *pro-
> vides altogether new* forms. . . .

> People for the most part (99 per cent of the bourgeoisie,
> 98 per cent of the Liquidators, some 60 to 70 per cent
> of the Bolsheviks) are unable to *think*, only able to
> *learn words by heart*. They have learned by heart the

[18] Lenin, XXXV, 232.

word "underground." Good. They can repeat it. This
they know by rote.

But *how its forms* must be changed under new circumstances, how one must learn *anew* for this, and how to
think, that we do not understand. . . .

I am greatly interested in knowing whether you could
explain this to the public. Write me in the greatest
detail. . . .[19]

No doubt in this "dialectical" and "statistical" analysis
of the class ability to think there is something intentionally
comic, but the complaint is serious all the same, and flattering in its implication that Inessa is one who can not only
think but perhaps write a pamphlet that will teach other
Bolsheviks how to think.

The year 1916 was a bitter, quarrelsome year for Lenin.
"Never, I think," wrote Krupskaya, "was Vladimir Ilyich
in a more irreconcilable mood than during the last months
of 1916 and the early months of 1917." "He had differences
of opinion with Rosa Luxemburg, Radek, the Dutch, Bukharin, Piatakov . . . and Kollontay" and even with his
sister Ann.[20] He wrote Inessa several letters full of abusive
reproaches of comrades who were closest to him, and apparently she reproved him in reply.

But just at that point, Maxim Gorky, who at his request was trying to arrange the legal publication of Lenin's
"Imperialism" in Petrograd, demanded that he omit some
of the epithets directed at Kautsky. This, Lenin wrote
Inessa, was "ridiculous and offensive"; then he added:
"There you are, that's my fate. One fighting campaign after
another—against political stupidities, vileness, opportunism,
etc. And this from 1893 on. And the hatred of the philistines
because of it. Well, all the same, I would not change my
fate for 'peace' with the philistines. . . ."[21]

[19] *Ibid.*, p. 96.
[20] Krupskaya, *op. cit.*, English edition, pp. 188 and 197; Russian, pp.
264-65 and 271. Lenin XXXV, 167.
[21] Lenin, XXXV, 209.

This is one of the rare autobiographical reflections we have from his usually extrovert pen.

His big opportunity to use Inessa, as we have already noted, came when he sent her in his place to represent the Bolsheviks at the International Socialist Bureau conference called in Brussels on July 16 and 17, 1914, to unify once more the Russian socialist movement. He was sending her to meet and do battle with such large figures as Kautsky, Vandervelde, Huysmans, Luxemburg, Plekhanov, Trotsky, and Martov. He counted on her mastery of all the languages of the International, her literal devotion to him and his views, her steadfastness under fire. Apparently Zinoviev or some other close lieutenant found Lenin's confidence misplaced and thought Inessa too small for the task, so he wrote her:

> I am convinced that you are one of those who develops, grows stronger, becomes more energetic and bolder when alone in a responsible post. . . . I stubbornly disbelieve the pessimists who say that you—are hardly —nonsense and again nonsense! With a splendid tongue you will smash them all; you will not let Vandervelde interrupt you and yell. . . .[22]

> You must make the report. You will say that you demand it and that you *have* precise and practical *proposals*. What can be more practical and businesslike? We go our way, they theirs—and we'll see what happens. Either a general line is accepted or we say let's report to our congress, *we to the congress of our party*. (But in fact, it is clear, we will accept exactly nothing.)[23]

After a great deal more in this vein, Lenin breaks into

[22] This did not prevent Lenin from writing out for her every word she was to say, and supplementing this with four sets of *zametki privées* (private notes). The report and instructions he wrote for her take up forty pages in Vol. XX of his *Sochineniia*.

[23] Lenin, XXXV, 108-10; XX, 463-502.

English, as he delights to do in his letters to this master of
five languages:

> *I've forgotten the money question. We will pay for
> letters, telegrams (please wire oftener) & railroad ex-
> penses, hotel expenses & so on. Mind it!**

> *If you succeed to receive the first rapport for 1-2 hours,
> it is almost all.**

> Then it remains to "kick back," to fish out their *con-
> trepropositions** (on all 14 points) and to declare *we
> do not agree* (not one of their proposals will we
> accept ...)*[24]

In all the forty pages of instructions and private notes,
although the time was nearly three weeks after the assassination of the Archduke at Sarajevo, Lenin has not one
word to say about war, except his own war against all the
other varieties of Russian socialism. Inessa, Krupskaya
writes, was selected because it was necessary to have a
firm person who could "resist a storm of indignation. . . .
She carried out her task bravely." And the police agent's
comment showed that she did so, to the "great disgust"
of the International Socialist Bureau representatives and
those from the other Russian factions, "as no one had expected the impudence of the Leninists to reach such pro-
portions."

To follow up Lenin's and their advantage, the police
instructed all their secret agents in the underground "stead-
fastly and persistently to defend the idea of the complete
impossibility of any organization fusion whatsoever . . .
especially a union of Bolsheviks and Mensheviks." Lenin,
who was taking no chances either, determined not to attend
the Emergency Session of the I.S.B. on July 29, 1914, the

---

[24] All passages in italics are underlined by Lenin in the original; an
asterisk (*) after them indicates that they are in English or French or
some other language than Russian. The first two paragraphs are in what
Lenin believes to be English, the third in Russian except for the word
contrepropositions.

day after Austria shelled Belgrade, for the sole purpose
of trying to stop the war from spreading.

We turn now to three letters to Inessa, one written on
June 5, 1914, and the other two in December, 1916, which
refer directly or indirectly to Inessa's preoccupation with the
"woman question," her reading in this field, and her plan
for a pamphlet.

The first deals with a novel by Vinenchenko, which
Inessa had recommended to Lenin, then sent him to read.
The novel was no doubt *The Commandments of Our
Fathers*.

> I have read, *my dear friend*,[25] the new novel by Vinen-
> chenko which you sent. What a nonsensical and stupid
> story!
>
> To bring together as many "horrors" as possible of all
> kinds, to collect and unite both "vice" and "syphilis"
> and romantic villainy, with extortion of money for a
> secret (and the transformation of the blackmail victim
> into a mistress) and the trial of a doctor! All with
> hysterics, mental contortions, pretensions to a theory
> of "his own" on the organization of prostitutes. . . .
>
> Coming singly, there are in life, of course, all the "hor-
> rors" which Vinenchenko depicts. But to join them all
> together. . . .
>
> Once I had to spend the night with a sick comrade
> (delirium tremens). And once I had to try to dissuade
> a comrade who was attempting suicide. In the end . . .
> he died a suicide. Both are memories *à la* Vinenchenko.
> But in each case these were small fragments of the
> lives of the two comrades. But this pretentious, arrant
> fool of a Vinenchenko . . . has made this a collection

[25] English in the original. Where the editors have not omitted the
salutation and closing, Lenin generally writes *Dorogoi Drug* (Dear
Friend) and closes with "firmly [or 'firmly, firmly'] I press your hand."
In one letter he tries to put this into English as "Friendly shake hands!"

of nothing but horrors. . . . Brrr—dullness, nonsense, unpleasant to have spent time in reading it.[26]

A glance at the novel will convince the reader that Lenin was the better critic and that Inessa's interest was largely due to the author's "own theory on the organization of prostitutes."

Unfortunately, Inessa's letter outlining her plan for a pamphlet on the "woman question" has not been published. But from Lenin's letters we can see that she had included among her list of "immediate demands" the "demand for free love." Pedantically, dogmatically, but with an effort to be tactful and gentle, Lenin sought to persuade her to strike it out. "This is really not a proletarian but a bourgeois demand," he writes in his first letter. "What *can* be understood by it?" Answering his own question, he enumerates ten possible interpretations:

> (1) Freedom from material calculations in the matter of love? (2) From material cares also? (3) From religious prejudices? (4) From prohibitions by papa, etc.? (5) From the prejudices of "society"? (6) From a narrow environment (peasant or petit-bourgeois-intellectual)? (7) From the fetters of law, the courtroom, and the police? (8) From the serious in love? (9) From childbirth? (10) Freedom of adultery?

> Of course, you have in mind not Nos. 8-10 but Nos. 1-7. . . . But for numbers 1-7 you must select another term, for free love does not exactly express this thought. And the public will *inevitably* understand by "free love" Nos. 8-10, just for the reason that it is not a proletarian but a bourgeois demand. . . . It is not a matter of what you "want to understand" *subjectively* by it. It is a matter of the *objective logic* of class relations in matters of love.[27]

Something in Lenin's letter—perhaps his remark on

[26] Lenin, XXXV, 107.
[27] *Ibid.*, pp. 137-38. This is the letter which closes with the English "Friendly shake hands!"

"freedom of adultery"—must have hurt Inessa deeply. In reply to her protest, not available to us, he defends his "class analysis" of love:

> Good, let us examine the question once more. . . .
> You "object": [you say] "I don't understand how it is POSSIBLE to identify (!!??) free love" with No. 10. So it seems that it is *I* who do the "identifying" and you are getting ready to scold . . . *me?*
> How? Why?
>
> *Bourgeois women* understand by free love pts. 8-10— that is my thesis. Do you reject that? Then tell me what *bourgeois* ladies do understand by free love? . . . Don't literature and life *prove* that? You must *mark yourself off* clearly from them, *oppose* to theirs the proletarian point of view. . . . Otherwise *they* will seize upon the corresponding points of your pamphlet, interpret them in their own way, make of your pamphlet water for their mill, pervert your thoughts before the workers, "confuse" the workers (by sowing among them the fear that the ideas *you* bring may be *alien* to them). And in their hands are the powerful hosts of the press.
>
> But, you, completely forgetting the objective and class point of view, pass over to an "attack" on *me*, as if it were *I* who "identify" free love with pts 8-10. Strange, verily, verily, strange . . .

Lenin seems to sense that this pedantic self-exculpation does not touch the core of her feeling, so he tries another approach:

> "Even a temporary passion and love affair"—so you write—is "more poetical and clean" than "kisses without love" of vulgar, and worse than vulgar, spouses. [The words I have rendered with "vulgar and worse than vulgar" are *poshlyi* (vulgar) and *poshlenkii,* a pejorative diminutive of the same word.—B.W.] So you write. And so you are getting ready to write in your pamphlet. Splendid.
>
> Is the contraposition logical? Kisses without love, of

vulgar spouses, is *dirty*. I agree. To this must be coun-
terposed—what? It would seem: kisses *with love?*

But you counterpose "temporary" (why temporary?)
"passion" (why not love?). Logically it turns out as
if kisses without love (temporary) are opposed to kisses
without love (conjugal) . . . Strange. For a popular
pamphlet, would it not be better to oppose to middle-
class-intellectual-peasant vulgar and dirty marriage
without love—proletarian, civil marriage with love
(with the addition, IF YOU ABSOLUTELY INSIST,
that a temporary affair-passion may also be dirty or
clean) . . .

Truly I do not want to engage in a polemic with you
at all. Gladly would I throw this letter away and post-
pone the matter until we can have a talk together.

But I did want your pamphlet to be a good one, so
that from it *no one would be able* to rip out a phrase
unpleasant for you. . . . I am sending you this letter
only that you may perhaps re-examine your plan in
more detail, as a result of letters, than on the occasion of a chat. A plan, you see, is a very important
thing. . . .[28]

The pamphlet was never written!

Inessa continued to play an important part in Lenin's
wartime activities. She served on the Bolshevik delegations to Zimmerwald and Kienthal. At the Berne Conference of Bolsheviks, she was one of a committee of three,
with Zinoviev and Lenin, that drafted the official resolution on war. (There is no doubt that the real author was
Lenin.) She continued to lead the Bolshevik work among
women. Despite her age—she was forty in 1914—she represented Bolshevism at the International Youth Conference.
She became one of the founders and a foreign editor of the
Petersburg legal Bolshevik journal, *The Woman Worker,*

[28] *Ibid.,* pp. 139-41.

the other editors being Kollontay (who agreed with her on "free love"), Lilina Zinoviev, Krupskaya, Lydia Stal, and Lenin's sister Anna.

Inessa was on the "sealed train" that took Lenin and his wife, the Zinovievs, and other prominent Bolsheviks back to Russia. Thereafter Lenin's life in the maelstrom of revolution, and hers, scarcely less agitated and active, in woman's work, work among French Communists and sympathizers in Russia, activities as first chairman of the Economic Council of Moscow Province, editor of the Woman's Section of *Pravda* and *Bednota,* her struggle against the ubiquitous prostitution during the years of civil war and economic breakdown, her translation work at two congresses of the Comintern—the churning whirlpool of revolution left little time for these two to think of themselves or each other.

The descriptions of her dating from this period agree that she dressed plainly, carelessly, even neglectfully, in worn and shabby garments; that she was ill fed, often cold and hungry; that her face had begun to show the ravages of overwork and neglect of self. At last, her friends and comrades, frightened by the signs of physical breakdown, persuaded her to go to the Caucasus for a rest. There too was hunger, overcrowding, floods of refugees, civil war, breakdown, disease. She slept in freight cars, was carried from town to town, and nursed the sick on the train. At last she was struck down herself by typhus in the autumn of 1920, dying at the age of forty-six.

When Alexandra Kollontay, then serving as ambassador to Norway, died in 1952, Marcel Body, a French communist who had been in Inessa's group in Moscow and then served as aide, intimate friend, and first secretary of Kollontay's embassy, wrote a memoir concerning the first woman ambassador in history. In the memoir he told how Kollontay had spoken to him of Lenin's deep love

for Inessa Armand.[29] Krupskaya had known of it, she said,
and in line both with the principles instilled in her by
Chernyshevsky's "uncommon persons" in *What's to be
Done?*, and the principles expressed in another favorite
tale of Lenin's, "The Story of Kolosov," by Turgenev,[30]
Krupskaya had bravely faced the thought that her husband
would now leave her for Inessa. When he did not go, she
offered to leave. More than once, she signified her inten-
tion of leaving, but each time Lenin said to her, "No,
stay!" Dutifully, she stayed.[31]

After Body published this memoir, Angelica Balabanoff felt that she too might break the puritanical silence

[29] Marcel Body, "Alexander Kollontai," in *Preuves* (Paris), April,
1952, pp. 12-24. Body was a French workingman, a printer in Limoges.
Mobilized in 1914, he was sent to Russia with a French military mission
to the Russian army. Like a number of other men of that mission (Captain
Jacques Sadoul, hitherto a Right Socialist, for example), he sympathized
with the February and October Revolutions. Remaining in Russia, he joined
first Inessa's group of French communists in Moscow, then the Russian
party, and served the Soviet government in various capacities. When
Kollontay arrived in Oslo as the world's first woman ambassador in 1922, a
kind of honorific exile by Lenin for her activity in the Workers Opposition,
she found Body there as secretary to Ambassador Suritz. His friendship
with her and his service under her began then and lasted until her death.
Sickened, as she was too, by Stalin's purges, he did not return to Russia
and now lives in Paris.

[30] "Kolosov" is the hero of a short tale by Turgenev, which Lenin
cherished as a discussion of the proper attitude of the "uncommon person"
toward love. Krupskaya told Valentinov that when they were in Siberia,
she and her husband translated several pages of the tale into German.
(This was Lenin's method of improving his German and at the same time
becoming more deeply acquainted with some of his favorite pages from
literature.) Kolosov, the narrator of the tale says, fell in love with a girl,
lost his love for her and left her. In this there was nothing "unusual."
Unusual was the resoluteness with which he broke with her and with his
whole past as tied up with her: "Which of us would have been able to
break in good time with his past? Who, say, who does not fear reproaches
—not, I say, the reproaches of the woman but the reproaches of the first
stupid bystander? Which of us would not yield to the desire to play the
magnanimous, or egotistically to play with another devoted heart? Finally,
which of us has the strength to oppose petty selfishness, petty proper feelings: pity and remorse? Oh, gentlemen, a person who breaks with a woman
once loved, at that bitter and great moment when he involuntarily realizes
that his heart is no longer entirely filled by her, that person, believe me,
better and more deeply understands the sacredness of love than do those
faint-hearted people who from tedium, from weakness, continue to play on
the half broken strings of their flabby and sentimental hearts. We all called
Andrei Kolosov an uncommon man. . . . In certain years, to be natural
means to be uncommon." (Cited by Valentinov, *op. cit.*, pp. 92-94.)

[31] Body, *op. cit.*, p. 17.

she had hitherto observed concerning Inessa in my many interviews with her on what she knew of Lenin.

> Lenin loved Inessa [Dr. Balabanoff told me]. There was nothing immoral in it, since Lenin told Krupskaya everything [again the same code]. He deeply loved music, and this Krupskaya could not give him. Inessa played beautifully—his beloved Beethoven and other pieces.

> He sent Inessa to the Youth Conference of the Zimmerwald Group—a little old, but she had a credential from the Bolsheviks and we had to accept it. He did not dare to come himself, sat downstairs in a little adjacent café drinking tea, getting reports from her, giving her instructions. I went down for tea and found him there. Did you come *na chai*, I asked, *ili na rezoliutsii?* (for tea, or for the resolution?) He laughed knowingly, but did not answer. [Inessa fought hard, but the resolution Lenin prepared for her was defeated 13-3.][32]

> When Inessa died, he begged me to speak at her funeral. He was utterly broken by her death. She died miserably of typhus in the Caucasus. I did not want to speak because I did not feel close to her nor really know her well. Yet I did not want to refuse.

> Fortunately, at the last moment, Kollontay arrived, and delivered a moving address. I cast sidelong glances at Lenin. He was plunged in despair, his cap down over his eyes; small as he was, he seemed to shrink and grow smaller. He looked pitiful and broken in spirit. I never saw him look like that before. It was something more than the loss of a "good Bolshevik" or a good friend. He had lost some one very dear and very close to him and made no effort to conceal it.

> He had had a child by Inessa. She married the German communist, Eberlein, who was purged by Stalin. What happened to Lenin's daughter then I do not know.[33]

[32] O. H. Gankin and H. H. Fisher, *The Bolsheviks and the World War* (Stanford, 1940), pp. 301-8, gives an account of this conference.

[33] The writer interviewed Angelica Balabanoff many times concerning

This last belief of Dr. Balabanoff, which I heard also from Germans who had known Hugo Eberlein well, is nevertheless mistaken. When Inessa died, the Ulyanovs adopted her daughter, Ina, and took her to live with them. It was at Lenin's home that Eberlein met Ina Armand, but she would have been too young to have been at a nubile age then if she had really been a daughter of Lenin and Inessa, whose personal acquaintance dates from 1910.[34] (Eberlein married for the second time in Moscow in 1921.)[35]

For the rest, Kollontay's account and Balabanoff's confirm each other. The account of Kollontay reads: "When her body was brought from the Caucasus and we accompanied her to the cemetery, Lenin was unrecognizable. He walked with closed eyes; at every moment we thought he would collapse." Always the romantic, Kollontay added: "He was not able to go on living after Inessa Armand. The death of Inessa hastened the development of the sickness which was to destroy him."

Be that as it may (he managed to continue active political life for two extremely full years, then died in the same way as his father, whom he so greatly resembled, at almost the same age), both accounts make it clear that Lenin deeply loved Inessa and that her death affected him profoundly.

To Krupskaya fell the task of writing the obituary notice for the Woman's Section of *Pravda*, on October 3, 1920. She tried hard to summon up a sense of loss, but the obituary is formless and colorless. In time, however, this devoted woman learned to accept this aspect of her hus-

Lenin during her years in America, but she never hinted at the Inessa affair until I said to her in Rome that I had learned of it from Marcel Body. Then she told me the above, permitting me to take notes as she talked.

[34] Singularly, most of the Ulyanov family of Lenin's generation, his sisters Anna and Maria, and Lenin himself, remained childless.

[35] On this see Ypsilon, *Pattern for World Revolution* (Chicago and New York, 1947), p. 68. The writer interviewed both of the anonymous authors of Ypsilon on Eberlein's marriage and Inessa Armand.

band's life, like every other, as parts of a paradigm of perfection. In 1926, Krupskaya edited and wrote the opening article of a symposium brochure, *In Memory of Inessa Armand*. It is the warmest and most informative essay in the collection. When in 1930-32 she came to write her *Memories of Lenin*, the personality of Inessa shone through its pages, radiant and joyous, as Lenin saw her. Thus perhaps it was Krupskaya, even more than Inessa and Lenin, who deserved the appellation of "uncommon person" used alike by Chernyshevsky and Turgenev in their discussions of freedom in love. Whatever may have been their reason, it was no longer Krupskaya's personal sensitiveness that motivated the Marx-Lenin Institute in waiting for her death before publishing the letters of Lenin to Inessa Armand. But the officials of the Institute did not know Krupskaya's spirit well enough to be aware of the change.

Perhaps we should add a footnote on the subsequent lives of the family of Inessa Armand. Her husband, after the loss of his fortune, entered "agriculture," working in a kolkhoz until his death in 1943. Her oldest son, Alexander, fought in the Civil War. For some reason which I have not been able to ascertain he was expelled from the Communist Party under Stalin shortly after World War II, thereafter having a difficult time. In 1957 he was reported to be working in the Thermotechnical Institute in Moscow. Fedor, her second son, was a military aviator, then engaged in the organization of athletics, until his death of tuberculosis in 1936. The youngest son, André, became an engineer and tank constructor. He died in battle in 1944.

The older daughter, Ina, lost her German communist husband in the Stalin blood purges. In 1957 she was working in the Marx-Lenin Institute. The younger daughter, Varvara, is a "decorative artist." At least, such is the account given in the official French communist biography of Inessa Armand. (All except the marriage to Eberlein and his subsequent purge, for unpersons did not then get into official biographies.)

APPENDIX

THE SOURCES I have used in the present study are the following: the references of Krupskaya (Lenin's wife) to Inessa in her *Vospominaniya o Lenine* (*Memories of Lenin*); Krupskaya's reminiscences concerning her, and the reminiscences of others of her friends, in *Pamyati Inessy Armand: Sbornik pod redaktsiei N. K. Krupskoi* (*In Memory of Inessa Armand: Symposium under the Editorship of N.K. Krupskaya*), Moscow, 1926; the letters of Lenin to Inessa, published in slightly censored form in Vol. XXXV of the Fourth Edition of his works; reminiscences of Angelica Balabanoff, communicated orally to the author; reminiscences of Marcel Body, French communist who recounted what he himself knew when Inessa was the organizer of the French communists in Moscow in 1918, and also what he learned from Alexandra Kollontay, as her confidant and aide in the Embassies of Norway and Sweden; a letter of Body to the writer; Jean Fréville, *Inessa Armand: Une Grande Figure de la Révolution Russe*, Paris, 1957 (Fréville was permitted to examine her letters and other materials in the archives of the Marx-Lenin Institute, but has refrained from quoting or been forbidden to quote from them); an obituary notice in *Pravda* written by Krupskaya on the occasion of Inessa's death; an article on her in the *Bolshaya Sovetskaya Entsiklopediia*; a discussion on her relations with Lenin in N. Valentinov, *Vstrechi s Leninym* (*Meetings with Lenin*), New York, 1953; Gérard Walter, *Lénine*, Paris, 1950.

These varying accounts contain some discrepancies, many reticences, and in some cases, palpable inaccuracies. Thus frequently her first name is given as Inessa (a pseudonym) and not Elizabeth. Her maiden name is omitted or wrongly given as Petrova, Petrovna (a pseudonym) or Stephanie (her father's stage name). Her father's stage name and real name are given in Lyonnet's *Dictionaire des Comédiens français*, Vol. II, p. 513.

8

The Double Agent

IN 1912, LENIN CALLED a conference in remote Prague to get away from the spies that seemed to be privy to his every activity. To Anton Nemec, Czech socialist leader, he made the plea: "Everything must be kept *ultra-conspirative.*" Krupskaya screened and interviewed each delegate, sending Brendinsky, whom she already suspected, on a wild goose chase to Brittany instead of Prague. The police took the hint, paying off their agent with a villa in a Paris suburb, costing forty thousand francs. But they were not too upset, for of the fourteen delegates coming from the Russian underground, two more, Romanov from Tula and Malinovsky from Moscow, were their men. Agent Malinovsky so captivated Lenin that he emerged a member of the new Central Committee and returned to his superiors with the exciting news that Lenin wanted him to run for the Duma.

If we were to list only the more important spies that had entered intimately into the life of Vladimir Ilyich by that time, the list would include Gurovich, who financed the first legal Marxist organ, *Nachalo,* with police funds; the surgeon dentist N. N. Mikhailov, who turned in Ul-

yanov, Martov, and the other organizers of the underground League for Struggle at the end of 1895; Dr. Jacob
Zhitomirsky, who, as Lenin's confidential agent in Berlin,
made the arrangements for Kamo and his case of dynamite,
for Krassin's counterfeit banknote paper, and for Litvinov's and other arrests in connection with the disposal of
the five-hundred-ruble notes of the Tiflis holdup. So well
did he work that Lenin continued to consider him as a
"man of confidence," to be used for the most delicate tasks.
After the Berlin arrests, Zhitomirsky moved "for safety"
to France, whence he visited Geneva in 1909 to urge
Vladimir Ilyich to move to Paris, "a large city where there
will be less spying." Writes Krupskaya: "The argument
was convincing to Ilyich." Thus the shadowed moved in
order to be closer to his shadow.

In 1911, Zhitomirsky finally fell under suspicion, but
it was not his chief who suspected him. Lenin received a
warning from Vladimir Burtsev. Now warnings from Burtsev were no small matter, for he was a self-constituted, one-
man, counter-espionage agency. As some collect coins or
stamps or feminine conquests, he collected spies. He it
was who shortly before had exposed the incomparable
Azev, director of the Fighting Section of the Social Revolutionary Party. Yet so sure was Lenin of his most trusted
agent that he ignored the warning.

A revolutionary bloodhound by vocation, Burtsev,
once he had scented a spy, was not to be put off the trail.
By 1913 he had gathered so much evidence that he sent
Lenin an ultimatum. He would create a public scandal if
trust were not withdrawn from this man. "If my charges
are false, let him haul me before a revolutionary tribunal.
There he will prove his innocence or I my charges."

Alarmed at last, Lenin sent another "man of confidence" to take up the Zhitomirsky matter with Burtsev,
and, at the same time, to discuss the whole problem of
combatting the spies with which the Bolshevik movement

was now obviously infested. The man whom Lenin sent
was Roman Malinovsky!

Malinovsky questioned Burtsev with strained interest.
Who in the police or the government was giving him his
secret tips? what reasons had he for suspecting Dr. Zhitomirsky? how could the Bolsheviks judge the reliability of
such grave charges unless they were given the sources?
what other Bolsheviks did he suspect? Insistently, Malinovsky pleaded that Burtsev communicate "in strict confidence" his sources in the government. For his part, Burtsev
had not the slightest reason to suspect his interlocutor,
whom he knew as a prominent trade unionist, as a member of the Central Committee which the Bolsheviks had
just set up allegedly as the Central Committee of the
entire Party, and as the newly chosen chairman of the
Bolshevik fraction in the Fourth Imperial Duma. Yet an
old habit of caution and a respect for confidences caused
him to withhold the names of the officials.

> I will give you two or three names of agents in
> your midst [he told the Duma Deputy with a pardon-
> able flourish]. Check them. Check the names of people
> arrested and their last contacts with men I name. If
> you are successful, I shall speak further . . .

In 1917, when the Tsar fell and the Provisional Government opened up the police archives, they found proof
that Zhitomirsky had been a spy during all the years he
enjoyed Lenin's confidence. This, of course, was no surprise to Burtsev. But what did startle him was the realization that Malinovsky (whom he did not even begin to
suspect until the end of 1916) had come to him that day
on a double mission, charged simultaneously by Vladimir
Ilyich and by the director of the Russian Police, S. P.
Beletsky, with the task of finding out which spies Burtsev
knew of in the Bolshevik faction, and from what government personages he derived his tips concerning these most

jealously guarded secrets of the police. How deep must Malinovsky's personal interest have been in learning Burtsev's secret, and knowing what revelations or whose turn was coming next!

Before we go on with our story, we must note a version, less flattering to Burtsev, of his interview with Malinovsky. The account we have just given is Burtsev's own, but from the well-informed Boris Nikolaevsky, biographer of Azev, who had many interviews with Burtsev, I got an account less favorable to the famous counter-espionage specialist. According to Nikolaevsky, Burtsev did not come to suspect Zhitomirsky as a result of his own investigations, but merely received a tip, couched in general terms, that someone very close to Lenin was a police agent. The tip came from Syrkin, a liberal official high in the Tsar's secret police, who offered to give details to someone whom he could trust. Thereupon, Burtsev wrote to Lenin asking him to come himself or send a man of absolute confidence, to whom he would divulge an important secret. When Lenin sent Roman Malinovsky, Burtsev confided to him that Syrkin of the Moscow Okhrana would give him the name of a police spy close to Lenin. Malinovsky took no chances. Instead of going to Syrkin, he reported the latter's offer to the chief of the Moscow Okhrana. Syrkin was dismissed from his post and exiled to Siberia.

What follows has been reconstructed by me from the police archives as published by the Provisional Government of 1917 and by the subsequent Soviet Government, and from the testimony of Roman Malinovsky's Party and police superiors before the Extraordinary Commission of the Provisional Government which investigated the Ministry of the Interior and its police in 1917.

Among those who testified before the Extraordinary Investigating Commission were former Minister of the Interior Makarov; Assistant Minister Zolotarev; the latter's

successor, Assistant Minister Junkovsky; Police Director
Beletsky; Assistant Director Vissarionov; Chief of the Moscow Okhrana Martynov; and other lesser officials. Citizens
Burtsev, Ulyanov (Lenin) and Radomyslsky (Zinoviev)
were summoned to testify before a special subcommission on the Malinovsky case. All the testimony before
the main investigating commission was stenogrammed and
subsequently published by the Soviet Government in a
seven-volume work called *The Fall of the Tsarist Regime.*
The testimony of Citizens Ulyanov and Radomyslsky before the subcommission were not so published, but I have
been able to reconstruct the text from contemporary accounts in the daily press: *Pravda* (Bolshevik), *Rabochaya
Gazeta* (Menshevik), *Den* (Liberal), and *Vestnik Vrem-
ennago Pravitelstva* (Official News Bulletin of the Provisional Government). Fortunately, this last contains a fair
amount of direct quotation in its issue of June 16, 1917, the
accuracy of which is confirmed by the reports in the other
dailies, including Lenin's *Pravda.* Other sources are the
writings of Burtsev, personal reminiscences of men who
knew Malinovsky, and documents summarized from memory by Boris Nikolaevsky, who was director of the Historical Archives of the Russian Revolution in Moscow during
the years 1919-21, that is, under the Soviet Government
at a time when Lenin was alive and active in the leadership of its affairs. Except where otherwise noted, the
source is always the seven-volume publication by the
Soviet Government of the stenogram of testimony before
the Extraordinary Commission of the Provisional Government.

From these sources we can reconstruct the amazing
life and deeds of Roman Malinovsky, as well as the political line pursued by the Police Department in the Bolshevik Faction, the Duma, and the Social Democratic
Party. For, as is characteristic of Russian officials, the Department had a definite political line.

Roman Vatslavovich Malinovsky was a Russified
Polish workingman of peasant stock, born in the Plotsk
Province of Russian Poland in the year 1878. When he
met Lenin at the Prague Conference of 1912, he was
thirty-four, robust, ruddy complexioned, vigorous, excit-
able, a heavy drinker, a rude and eloquent orator, a gifted
leader of men. In the closing years of the preceding century he had been convicted several times of common
crimes, the third offense being that of robbery with breaking and entry, for which he had served a prison term from
1899 to 1902. The police noted that he was a heavy spender.
Though he earned a living first as tailor and then as metal
turner, his wages were never sufficient for his expensive
tastes. In his youth he had worked for a while in Germany,
then returned to Saint Petersburg. Here he entered the
labor movement, probably in 1902, with a perfect background for the role of police informer.

How early he became a regular agent is unclear. For
years his chief source of income was his wages as a metal
worker, while he used his police connections only to pick
up a bit of extra cash. When he thought he had something
which would interest them, he would telephone, or send
in a written report signed *Portnoi* ("Tailor"), for which he
would be paid a sum like twenty-five or fifty rubles. Even
after he became a professional agent with a regular salary,
he did not become a "professional revolutionist"—his use-
fulness consisted in his continuing to be a worker at the
bench. He himself was to confess to the Bolsheviks, and
the police were to confirm, that one of his motives was
always the ambition to rise to a place of prominence in
the revolutionary movement. This ambition felt a double
spur: the higher his advancement, the more he meant to
the police and the higher the sum they set on the value of
his services.

In 1906 he was one of the founders of the Petersburg
Metal Workers Union. In 1907 he became its secretary,
serving till the end of 1909. Here he steered a careful

course between Bolsheviks and Mensheviks. The former were more interested in control and political leadership of the union, the latter in the preservation of its autonomy. Therefore, as an active unionist, he inclined to the Mensheviks. In 1908 he successfully resisted an attempt of the Bolsheviks to capture his union, but, after he went over to them completely, he helped them to win control. Zinoviev, who met him while he was the union's secretary, testified to the Extraordinary Commission that he thought him to be "rather a Menshevik," and the Mensheviks had the same opinion.

Five times he was arrested by the police for his activities, either because they had no inkling of his role, or because he was at a meeting which he himself had betrayed, where everybody had to be taken in. His early reappearance on the scene after each arrest was so managed as not to excite suspicion. A typical arrest was that of late November, 1909. He had tipped off a secret caucus of the labor delegates to an impending anti-alcoholic congress and was present when it was raided. Released in January, 1910, he was exiled from Saint Petersburg to avert suspicion from him. This ended his secretaryship of the Petersburg union, but he immediately turned up in Moscow in the spring of 1910, where he was welcomed by the entire labor movement and was able to report to the police on every phase of it. On the rolls of the Moscow Okhrana he appears as of March, 1910, no longer as a "piece worker," but with the regular salary of fifty rubles a month, plus expenses. In addition, of course, to his wages as a metal turner.

The police had come to the conclusion that the chief danger to the régime was the possible unification of all opposition forces against it:

> Malinovsky was given the order to do as much as possible to deepen the split in the Party. [Testimony of Police Director Beletsky, Stenogram Vol. III, p. 281.]

> I admit that the whole purpose of my direction is
> summed up in this: to give no possibility of the Party's
> uniting. I worked on the principle of *divide et impera*.
> [*Ibid.*, p. 286.]

Since this political aim coincided in an essential respect with that of Lenin, Malinovsky was now instructed
to take the earliest possible opportunity to come out as a
Bolshevik and to attach himself as closely as possible to
the Bolshevik leader. Police Director Beletsky testified
that, in view of this important mission, he freed his agent
at this time from the further necessity of betraying individuals or meetings (though not from reporting on them),
as arrests traceable to Malinovsky might endanger his
position for the more highly political task. It was the
easier for the police to make this exemption since they had
by now advanced their men to a number of key posts in
the Bolshevik underground, including the headship of the
Moscow organization itself, which had just been taken
over by agent Kukushkin, aided by the spies Romanov,
Poskrebuchin and Marakushev. The agents ascended
quickly in the Party hierarchy by the simple expedient of
arranging the arrest of incumbents, persons who suspected
them, and others who stood in their way.

But Malinovsky seemed to enjoy denunciatory work,
and, despite the exemption, continued it. Indeed, he could
not resist one more grand coup before he went to the
Bolsheviks. As a leading official of a legal trade union, he
was highly esteemed by the "Liquidators" who set their
hopes on legal unions and the legalization of other mass
activities, and found Lenin's underground a hindrance.
Malinovsky helped with the conference which was to plan
the fight for legality, then tipped off Police Chief Beletsky
to raid the planning committee. Most of the "Liquidators"
were bagged and their hopes ended for some time to come.
Thus the police aided Lenin against the "Liquidators,"
while agent Brendinsky was clearing another obstacle

from Lenin's path by arranging for the arrest of the Conciliator Bolshevik Rykov. In the retrospective light of the 1917 police testimony, all of Lenin's and Malinovsky's subsequent polemics against the Liquidators as "police agents," "police unionists," and "advocates of a police labor party" make strange reading indeed. Beletsky's testimony on the raid on the Liquidators is confirmed by a note in the official edition of Vol. XVII of Lenin's *Collected Works:*

> Malinovsky clearly did not break with the Liquidators completely. He took part in a conference of their supporters, and played his hand in such fashion that the conference, called by them for the fall of 1911, was raided by the police. At that time a suspicion arose in a narrow circle of Moscow workers and Social Democrats who were in contact with Malinovsky . . . but the rumors concerning him soon died down.

About the same time, Malinovsky learned that Lenin was summoning a Party conference too, at which he was to "remove" the Central Committee regularly elected by the last united party congress, and set up in its place a Bolshevik-dominated central committee. The conference, as we know, was held in Prague in January, 1912. Malinovsky appeared as the representative of the Moscow trade unions and of the Bolshevik underground political organization, of which his fellow-agent Kukushkin was the head. Lenin had of course heard of this well-known trade unionist, newly won from Menshevism. As we know, he was so taken with the convert that Malinovsky was elected to the new Central Committee, and was urged to become the Party's standard-bearer in the contest for a Duma deputyship from Moscow

A police spy with a record of convictions for common crimes as a Duma Deputy—the idea was so audacious that the highest authorities had to be consulted. Now Beletsky met with his agent only in private rooms of fashionable

restaurants. He claims that he took his agent in person to
see the Minister of the Interior, consulted with the Assistant Police Chief, the Assistant Interior Minister, the head
of the Moscow Okhrana, the Governor of Moscow, Junkovsky. The testimony of these persons before the Investigating Committee of the Provisional Government is often contradictory. It is probable that Junkovsky, when he claims
not to have known, was telling the truth, for it was he who
finally caused the dismissal of Malinovsky. In any case,
many in high places knew the secret.

Interdepartmental communications on the subject
were now so cautious that they no longer referred to their
agent by his old pseudonym of *Portnoi*, but each used
such circumlocutions as "the personage of whom I spoke
to Your Excellency on such and such occasion."

Both police and Bolsheviks set to work with great
energy to secure their candidate's nomination and election.
The newly founded daily *Pravda*, the Bolshevik apparatus,
and—what proved more important—the whole machinery
of the Department of the Interior and its police were
mobilized to further Malinovsky's fortunes. The first
hurdle was his criminal record. The Ministry saw to it
that he got the necessary "certificate of good repute" from
local authorities in his native province. Next, all the more
popular of his possible rivals were eliminated by the
simple expedient of throwing them into jail. This included
the most likely candidate of the Moscow workers, Krivov.

As election day approached, Malinovsky reported
that a hostile foreman was planning to fire him from his
factory. The electoral system provided for workingmen to
vote by secret ballot in their factories, where they chose
delegates to the next higher nominating body, which in
turn chose electors for the Workers' Curiae of the Provincial Electoral College, where actual selection of Deputies
was made. (Thus neither voting in the factories nor in-
direct elections are Soviet inventions, as is so widely

believed, but were inherited from tsarism.) But no workingman was eligible to vote or to be chosen as delegate,
elector, or Deputy unless he had worked in the given factory for the six months preceding the election. The Police
Department came to their candidate's rescue once more
by throwing the astonished foreman into jail, releasing
him after the elections with the explanation that the arrest
had been "an unfortunate mistake." (Neither in tsarist nor
in Soviet Russia has there ever been any recourse against
officials for false arrest.) Aided by such campaign
methods, the Bolshevik and police joint candidate swept
all before him. The Department showed its appreciation
of his advancement in the secular world by raising his
salary from fifty rubles a month to five hundred. It was the
first time that any police spy ever got such princely salary.
And this was now supplemented not by a metal worker's
wage but by a Duma Deputy's.

> *For the first time* among ours in the Duma [wrote
> Lenin in a letter full of the underscorings with which
> he showed his excitement] there is an *outstanding*
> worker-*leader.* He will read the Declaration [the po-
> litical declaration of the Social Democratic fraction on
> the address of the Prime Minister]. This time it's not
> another Alexinsky. And the results—perhaps not imme-
> diately—will be *great. . . .*

The Fourth Imperial Duma, to which Malinovsky was
elected, began its term in late November, 1912. It was to
be a long Duma, destined to continue in being until the
Revolution of 1917 thrust power into its reluctant hands.
Its thirteen Social Democratic Deputies (seven Mensheviks and six Bolsheviks) formed a single Fraction, for the
split which Lenin had started abroad at the Prague Conference at the beginning of that year had not yet taken
effect inside Russia. The Fraction chose Chkheidze, Georgian Menshevik and leader of the Georgian revolutionary

armed forces in 1905, as chairman, and Malinovsky as
vice-chairman, and commissioned the latter to read the
first political declaration.

Lenin was highly displeased with this unity in the
Duma Fraction, for, as long as it endured, here was an
authoritative and conspicuously public leading body
around which the longing for unity inside Russia might
crystallize, as against the Prague (Bolshevik) Central
Committee. So strong was "conciliationism," i.e. the mood
for unity, that the six Bolsheviks had gotten elected only
by pledging themselves to work for a united party. Thus
the entire bloc of Deputies lent their names as contribut-
ing editors both to the Bolshevik legal daily, *Pravda*, and
the Menshevik daily, *Luch*, and four of the six Bolsheviks
even signed a call for the fusion of the two papers. Indeed,
from reading them, one could not then deduce any very
good reason for their remaining separate, for Lenin was
having great trouble with his editors. *Pravda* had been
founded on the eve of the election campaign to take advantage of the increasing liberality of the government with
reference to the press. The better to direct it, Lenin had
moved from Paris to Kracow in Austrian (Polish) Galicia,
only a day and a night by express from Saint Petersburg.

Despite the closer contact, *Pravda* continued to assume a "Conciliator" attitude in response to the popular
mood inside Russia. It went so far as to censor, mutilate,
or suppress Lenin's articles where they sought to sharpen
the fight against Mensheviks, Liquidators, Bundists, and
Vperyodists.

> Vladimir Ilyich was so upset when from the out-
> set *Pravda* deliberately struck out from his articles all
> polemics with the Liquidators . . . Ilyich became nerv-
> ous, wrote irate letters to *Pravda*, but they did not do
> much good . . . [writes Krupskaya].

Here are excerpts from some of his "irate letters":

> We received a stupid and impudent letter from the

Editorial Board. We will not reply. They must be kicked out . . . We are exceedingly upset by the absence of plans for reorganizing the Board . . . Better yet, complete expulsion of all the veterans . . . They praise the Bund and *Zeit,* which is simply despicable. They don't know how to proceed against *Luch,* and their attitude toward my articles is monstrous . . . [Letter of Jan. 12, 1913.]

We must kick out the present editorial staff . . . Would you call such people editors? They aren't men but pitiful dishrags, who are ruining the cause. . . . [Letter of Jan. 20.]

And to Gorky:

And how did *you* happen to get mixed up with *Luch*??? Is it possible that you are following in the footsteps of the Deputies? But they have simply fallen into a trap!

At the time these angry letters were written, Stalin was in Saint Petersburg and Molotov was secretary of the Editorial Board. The fact that they were on the receiving end of these bursts of anger probably explains why Stalin's *History of the Communist Party of the Soviet Union* eliminated all traces of the quarrel.

As early as December 18, 1912, that is to say a few days after the Duma Fraction was organized, the astute Malinovsky was able to report to his superiors the news that he would be able to split the Fraction and would have Lenin's support for this purpose. On that date Assistant Police Director Vissarionov wrote to the Minister of the Interior:

The situation of the Fraction is now such that it may be possible for the six Bolsheviks to be induced to act in such a way as to split the Fraction into Bolsheviks and Mensheviks. Lenin supports this. See his letter.

The letter referred to, a copy of which Malinovsky

supplied to Vissarionov, was one Lenin had written a few days earlier to "Vassiliev" (the name then being used by Stalin). It had been written in invisible ink between the lines of a commercial letter to an official of the Russian Bank for Foreign Trade.

> If all of our six are from the Workers' Curiae [said the secret writing] they cannot silently submit to a lot of Siberians. The six must come out with the sharpest protest if they are being majorityized [*mayoriziruyut*, i.e. being overridden by the seven], they should publish a protest in *Pravda* and announce that they are appealing to the ranks, to the workers' organizations.

This was to be the gist of Lenin's argument and of Malinovsky's strategy for disrupting the united Fraction. Malinovsky of Moscow, Badaev of Saint Petersburg, and the other Bolsheviks from Tula and lesser centers, all six in short, had been chosen by the Workers' Curiae, ran Lenin's argument. Not one of the Menshevik Deputies had come from a Workers' Curia; thus the Georgian Mensheviks, for example, had been elected by the entire Georgian population. Therefore the Bolshevik six must be regarded as representing a majority of the working class and the Menshevik seven a minority. They were not representatives of the industrial working class, but "a lot of Siberians." It was a curious foreshadowing of the argument of 1918 concerning the superior representative character of the Soviets as against the Constituent Assembly.

Finding Malinovsky able and willing ("the other Bolshevik Deputies," writes Krupskaya, "were shy, but it was quite obvious that they were good, reliable proletarians"), Lenin left to him the task of finding pretexts for leading the Bolshevik Duma group toward an open break with the Mensheviks, while he himself turned his attention to *Pravda*. He called Stalin to Kracow to instruct him on the matter, and sent Jacob Sverdlov, his best organizer, to

Saint Petersburg to whip the editors into line. Soon he was able to write gratefully to Sverdlov:

> Today we learned about the beginning of reforms on *Pravda*. A thousand greetings, congratulations and good wishes for success . . . You cannot imagine how tired we are of working with a completely hostile editorial staff. [Letter of Feb. 8, 1913.]

Malinovsky dutifully reported the arrival of Sverdlov. He hid in Duma Deputy Petrovsky's home, but was arrested when he left there to "move to a safer place" (Feb. 10, 1913). Thereupon Lenin dispatched Stalin, now fully prepared to carry out the splitting or "irreconcilable" line, to Saint Petersburg. On March 13, after confiding his plans for that night to Malinovsky, Stalin went to a concert for the benefit of *Pravda*, where he too was arrested. Both Sverdlov and Stalin were sent to Siberia. This time they stayed, all through the war, until released by the Revolution of February, 1917.

Next Kamenev was sent to take charge. The mood of Lenin's household when Kamenev left is reflected in this passage from Krupskaya's memoirs:

> We all [Inessa Armand, the Zinovievs, Krupskaya and Lenin] went to the station to see them off . . . We spoke very little. Every one was wrapped up in his own thoughts. We all asked ourselves how long Kamenev would hold out, how soon we should meet again? When would we be able to go to Russia? Each of us secretly thought about Russia; each of us had a strong desire to go. Night after night I would dream of the Nevsky Gate [a suburb of Saint Petersburg]. We avoided speaking on the subject but all of us secretly thought about it . . .

Unexpectedly, Kamenev's stay was made legal by an act of the government: an amnesty for all "literary political" offenders, decreed to celebrate the three-hundredth anniversary of the founding of the Romanov dynasty. So,

instead of turning Kamenev in, Malinovsky provided him
with excellent copy by fiery denunciation of his Menshevik fellow-Deputies. The new line found a willing supporter in the new editor-in-chief of *Pravda*, Miron Chernomazov, another police agent. In October, 1913, Lenin
expressed his satisfaction to Kamenev on *Pravda's* line:

> Here everybody is satisfied with the newspaper
> and its editor [doubtless, Kamenev is meant, for he
> was the real behind-the-scenes editor]. In all this
> time I haven't heard a single word of criticism.

And Lenin had every reason to be satisfied. The
Duma Fraction had split at last. The mellow mood of conciliationism had vanished. *Pravda* was engaged in daily
"merciless and irreconcilable war" with both Menshevik
tendencies (now all lumped together as "Liquidators"),
the Bundists, and the Trotskyite "non-factionalists." Most
of the Vperyodists had abandoned their independent
standard and either gone over to Trotsky's league of party-
unity advocates or had returned, repentant, to the Leninist
fold.

The police, too, were satisfied. Yet this business of
having the Bolshevik leader of the Duma on their payroll
was bringing its complications. First, there were his
speeches. He was undeniably eloquent and forceful. Sometimes Malinovsky wrote them himself and sent them to his
two chiefs, Lenin and Beletsky, for approval. At other
times Lenin or Zinoviev or Kamenev drafted them, or even
wrote out whole speeches in detail. These, too, were sent
to Police Chief Beletsky for his opinion. In the police files
were found drafts in Malinovsky's hand, with amendments
in the handwriting of both Lenin and Beletsky, as well as
drafts by Lenin, Zinoviev, and Kamenev. Realizing how
popular their Deputy was, the police tried to cut out
some of the most "subversive" passages. But Malinovsky
had difficulty following instructions. In reading the first

declaration of the Fraction, he managed to eliminate an offending passage on "sovereignty of the people" by pretending to get rattled and skipping an entire page of his manuscript. But *Pravda* and *Luch* next day followed his original script. When his speeches were attacks on the Liberals, Constitutional Democrats (Kadets), or Mensheviks, the police were glad to give him full rein. Sometimes he tried to substitute a belligerent "revolutionary" fight with Duma Chairman Rodzyanko for the delivery of the speech itself, thus managing to get himself interrupted and denied the right to continue. Yet, on the whole, the Leninist régime so closely limited the autonomy of a Deputy and of the Duma Fraction that the police had little success in modifying his speeches. Without doubt he enjoyed both roles and there must have been moments when he thought of himself as a Bolshevik doublecrossing the police rather than a police agent spying on the Bolsheviks. So Azev had become confused as to his double role, and Father Gapon, and the Bundist police agent Kaplinsky, who as the "Azev" of the Bund plotted many acts of terror and denounced many terrorists to the police, but conscientiously refused to inform on a single member of the Bund! And so Dmitri Bagrov, who murdered Stolypin under such circumstances that it could never be disentangled whether it was on the order of revolutionaries, on the behest of some other official, or to avenge the pogroms against Jews for which Bagrov, wrongfully, held Stolypin responsible. There was something in the Russian temperament and scene that engendered these men of ambivalent spirit and double role, these Gapons, Azevs, Kaplinskys, Bagrovs, and Malinovskys—figures without parallel in the police and revolutionary movements of other lands.

Another complication was the danger of exposure. Some official high in the Ministry of the Interior or the Police was privy to the arrangement and did not like it. From the outset, this still today unknown personage tried to communicate with the socialist "underworld" without revealing his identity. When Malinovsky was elected, *Luch* received an anonymous warning on his role. A year later the wife of the socialist leader Theodor Dan received a letter telling her that a high police official wanted to see her in confidence, and that she could signify acceptance of the appointment by a code advertisement in a stipulated newspaper. Both warnings were ignored.

When Bukharin, living in Vienna, learned of Malinovsky's election, he wrote to Lenin that he had escaped from exile in 1910 only to be seized again in Moscow, suspiciously, right after a meeting with Malinovsky. He was puzzled by the angry tone of Lenin's answer: there was a dark campaign of slander being waged against this wonderful Bolshevik; if Bukharin joined it, Lenin would brand him publicly as a traitor. He desisted.

Then there were the February and March, 1913, arrests of Elena Rozmirovich (Mrs. Troyanovsky), Sverdlov, and Stalin. Acting on a hunch, Troyanovsky wrote from abroad a "shot-in-the-dark" letter to his wife's relatives in which he said that he knew who had caused her arrest: "a man playing a double role." If she were not freed, he would make an exposure which would "stagger society." As Troyanovsky had calculated, the police opened the letter. Director Beletsky testified in 1917 that when he had shown the letter to Malinovsky the latter had "become hysterical" and demanded her release as a condition for serving the Department further. She was released.

To ward off suspicion, Malinovsky declared at a meeting of the Central Committee that "someone close to the Duma Six was a person who had police connections." The axe fell on agent Miron Chernomazov, already under investigation, in February, 1914; he was quietly removed from the editorial board of *Pravda*. He had been its editor-in-chief while Malinovsky was its treasurer. The latter position enabled the Duma Deputy to turn in copies of the paper's balance sheet, and a complete list of the names and addresses of all who contributed money. On the other hand, he held meetings, raised funds for the paper, contributed himself from time to time—amounts which he always added to his Police Department expense accounts. These sums the police more than recouped when they levied fines on the paper, in one case a fine of five hundred rubles for an article written by none other than Duma Deputy Malinovsky.

During all this time Malinovsky was practically a commuter between Kracow and Petersburg. Aided both by police and Bolshevik underground, it was easy for him to cross the frontier. Lenin summoned him at every important juncture, giving him entry into the most highly confidential meetings, when the only other persons present were Lenin and Krupskaya, Zinoviev, and Kamenev. The Police Department received full transcripts of the decisions taken, all Lenin's most secret acts and plans. Every biographer and historian owes a debt to these complete and competent police reports for the period. Malinovsky went on joint lecture tours with Lenin to all the Russian colonies in emigration. Together they attended a secret congress of the Lettish Social Democrats and another of the Finns. He was entrusted with setting up a secret printing plant inside Russia, which naturally did not remain secret for long. Together with Yakovlev he "helped" start a Bolshevik paper in Moscow. It, too, ended promptly with the arrest of the editor. Inside Russia, the popular Duma Deputy traveled to all centers. Arrests took place sufficiently later to avert suspicion from him. Thus a Bolshevik "Conciliator" group headed by Miliutin disappeared, as did the regular Bolshevik organization in Tula and other local bodies. The police raised his wage from five hundred to six hundred, and then to seven hundred rubles a month.

On the 8th of May, 1914, Roman Malinovsky handed in his resignation to the Chairman of the Duma, Rodzyanko, "for reasons of health," and the same day left the country. He had notified neither Central Committee nor

Duma Fraction nor constituents. The amazement at this inexplicable action was enormous. At each session of the Duma, whenever a Bolshevik arose to speak, the reactionary Deputy Markov would cry out with intentioned malice: *"But where is Malinovsky?"*

The leaderless Fraction—for the others were smallish figures who had let Malinovsky guide the day-to-day struggle with the Mensheviks—reviewed the events leading up to his disappearance in an effort to find a key to the mystery. Recently he had been quick-tempered, more so even than usual. He had complained of his health, and of wearying with "mere parliamentary means of struggle." On April 22, the new Chairman of the Council of Ministers, the reactionary Goremykin, aroused a storm in the Duma by warning the Socialist spokesman, Chkheidze, against using the Duma for radical attacks on the government. Deputies pounded their desks; Chkheidze and Chkhenkeli had to be dragged out by guards; both Social Democrats and Trudoviks were suspended by Chairman of the Duma, Rodzyanko, for fifteen days. Malinovsky tried to persuade the ousted deputies that it would be "shameful to return to the Duma." But on May 7, he returned with the rest of the Deputies. One by one they attempted to read into the minutes a statement of protest, and one by one they were silenced and declared out of order by Chairman Rodzyanko. When Malinovsky got the floor, he seemed to be beside himself. He refused to be silenced, continuing to shout until the sergeant-at-arms was called to remove him from his seat. Again he urged all Left deputies to resign and "appeal to the people." Next day he went to the astonished Rodzyanko and handed him his resignation.

That same day, Chairman Rodzyanko received a visit from Assistant Minister of the Interior Junkovsky, who informed him, "in strict confidence," that the departed Deputy had been a police agent and had been ordered to resign to avoid a possible scandal. Rodzyanko was told that he might inform the Presidium of the Duma, but that the secret should go no further, or the good name of the Duma itself would be compromised. The last police entry on Malinovsky was a dismissal bonus of six thousand rubles to start life anew abroad.

Now *Luch* remembered its old anonymous letter. Rumors swirled around the corridors of the Tauride Palace and soon the entire press was speaking of "dark police complications." But when Lenin's friend Bonch-Bruevich, as correspondent of the Kharkov daily *Utro*, sent a dispatch of the same tenor to his paper, he received a sharp telegram from Lenin categorically denying the allegation. For the ever reckless Malinovsky, despite the peril of his situation, had gone straight to Lenin in Cracow!

There he had given several contradictory "political" and "personal" versions of his flight. Then, on closer questioning, he had "confessed" that in his youth he had been sentenced for an attempt at rape, which fact the police now threatened to expose if the most useful of the Bolshevik Deputies did not resign from the Duma. While Lenin was pondering this, the Menshevik and Liquidator press arrived with their reports of rumors that the Bolshevik leader had been a police spy. Martov and Dan raised the question: was it not factionalism itself that enabled unreliable elements to rise so high in the Party? They demanded a non-factional or multi-factional Party tribunal to investigate the case, political and personal, of Roman Malinovsky. For Lenin, and for his faction now representing itself as the Social Democratic Party, the situation was fraught with potential disaster. To accept the proposal of Martov and Dan was to recognize that the "expelled" Mensheviks were still part of the Social Democratic Party. And what a weapon against Bolshevism would be provided by the thought that its outstanding spokesman, its leader inside Russia, the driving force of its campaign to split the Duma Fraction, was a police agent! What universal demoralization if this man who knew everybody, had trav-

eled everywhere, had had in his hands all connections, all
secret lists of members, sympathizers and contributors of
funds to *Pravda*, should turn out to be a spy!

In the name of the Party (i.e. the Bolshevik) Central
Committee, an investigating commission was immediately
set up. It consisted of Lenin, Zinoviev, and Hanecki, a
Polish Social Democrat of the Warsaw Opposition and a
close supporter of Lenin's. No Mensheviks were included.
This commission heard testimony from Malinovsky, from
Bukharin, who reiterated his old charges, from Mrs. Troyanovsky, who told the circumstances of her arrest and
release, and testified that her interlocutors had shown
knowledge of matters which, in her judgment, only Malinovsky could have told them. Burtsev was asked his opinion. He answered that he thought the Duma Deputy a
"dirty fellow but not a police agent."

Bukharin's reminiscences of that difficult moment
were published in *Pravda* on January 21, 1925, one year
after Lenin's death:

> I distinctly hear Ilyich walking downstairs. He
> does not sleep. He goes out on the terrace, prepares tea,
> and up and back he strides on the terrace. He strides
> and strides, stops and again strides up and down. Thus
> the night passes. . . .
>
> Morning. I go out. Ilyich is neatly dressed. Under
> his eyes are yellow circles. His face is that of an ill
> man. But he laughs gaily, the accustomed gestures, the
> accustomed sureness:
>
> "Well, what do you say, did you sleep well? Ha,
> ha, ha! Good. Want tea? Want bread? Let's go for a
> walk?" Just as if nothing had happened. Just as if
> there had not been a night of torture, suffering, doubt,
> cogitation, tense mental effort. No, Ilyich had donned
> the mail of his steel will. Was there anything that could
> break it?

That night, sentimentally remembered by Bukharin,

Lenin decided to exonerate Malinovsky of the main charge
against him, and to pronounce Martov and Dan "malicious
slanderers." When Bukharin's reminiscence appeared in
1925, Martov's paper took it to mean that Lenin, during
that tortured night, had knowingly decided to defend a
police spy and attack his accusers out of cold factional calculation. But the passage we have quoted is capable of
another interpretation: that Lenin had succeeded in convincing himself of the truth of the rape story and the
falsity of the police agent charge. Which interpretation is
correct? Let us examine the available evidence.

> Vladimir Ilyich thought it utterly impossible for
> Malinovsky to have been an *agent provocateur* [re-
> cords Krupskaya]. These rumors came from Menshevik
> circles . . . The commission investigated all the rumors
> but could not obtain any definite proof of the charge
> . . . Only once did a doubt flash across his mind. I
> remember one day in Poronino [the summer residence
> of the Ulyanovs where the trial took place], we were
> returning from the Zinovievs and talking about these
> rumors. All of a sudden Ilyich stopped on the little
> bridge we were crossing and said: "It may be true!"—
> and his face expressed anxiety. "What are you talking
> about, it's nonsense," I answered deprecatingly. Ilyich
> calmed down and began to abuse the Mensheviks, say-
> ing that they were unscrupulous as to the means they
> employed in the struggle against the Bolsheviks. He
> had no further doubts on the question.

"These rumors came from Menshevik circles . . ."
Here was the key to Lenin's reaction. The Bolshevik press
adopted a resolution condemning Malinovsky for "in-
discipline . . . desertion of his post . . . disorganizing departure . . . a crime which placed him outside the ranks
of the Social Democratic Party." And condemning "the
Liquidators" (Martov was now always treated as a Liquidator too) for "hurling dirty and malicious slanders at the
former Deputy, like the Rightist press which spreads

slanderous rumors in order to bring confusion into the ranks of the workers."

In the Bolshevik theoretical organ, *Prosveshchenie* (*Enlightenment*), Lenin published a long article directed not against Malinovsky but against Martov and Dan, under the title: "The Methods of Struggle of Bourgeois Intellectuals Against the Workers."

In it Dan and Martov are denounced as incurably gossipy old women who live for scandal ("like insects that defend themselves by secreting an evil-smelling fluid"). They are worse than "the other Liquidators." Martov's famous pamphlet against Lenin, *Saviors or Destroyers*, is retroactively denounced as another example of this "impermissible, dirty, slanderous method." To the proposal for an impartial court of investigation, Lenin answered:

> *We do not believe one single word* of Dan and Martov. We *will never* enter into any "investigation" of dark rumors in which the Liquidators and the grouplets which support them may take part . . . If Martov and Dan, plus their concealers, the Bundists, Chkheidze and Co., the "August Bloc People," etc., directly or indirectly invite us to a common "investigation," we answer them: we don't trust Martov and Dan. We do not regard them as honest citizens. We will deal with them only as common criminals—only so, and not otherwise . . . If a man says, make political concessions to me, recognize me as an equal comrade of the Marxist community or I will set up a howl about rumors of the provocateur activity of Malinovsky, that is political blackmail. Against blackmail we are always and unconditionally for the bourgeois legality of the bourgeois court . . . Either you make a public accusation signed with your signature so that the bourgeois court can expose and punish you (there are no other means of fighting blackmail), or you remain as people branded . . . as slanderers by the workers . . .

So far had the atmosphere been embittered since the

Unity Congresses of 1906 and 1907! The main steps toward this impasse had been the exposure of Lenin's responsibility for the revolutionary robberies (Martov's *Saviors or Destroyers*, 1911), Lenin's seizure of the Party apparatus at the Prague Conference (January, 1912), the maneuvers of Lenin and Malinovsky to smash the unified Duma Fraction (December, 1912, to October, 1913), and now the rumors that the Bolshevik Duma leader was a police agent. Lenin did not have enough faith in Martov and Dan as fellow Social Democrats to sit on a common committee with them. He refused to recognize either of them "as an equal comrade of the Marxist community." This embitterment, this factional momentum, was one of the incalculable component forces entering into the final split of 1917. Even the fact that Martov became a Menshevik Internationalist and Lenin a Bolshevik Internationalist could not bring them together during the World War, which both opposed.

A sifting of the evidence still leaves doubt in our minds. Did Lenin believe Malinovsky's story of an early conviction for attempted rape, and the resignation of his mandate under threat of exposure? Or did he decide "on balance" that a spy could still be useful?

> One feels ashamed for mankind [wrote Lenin on June 4, 1914] when one sees how a man's personal misfortune is utilized for a struggle against an opposing political tendency.

That was a little over a month before the war began. Lenin's treatment of Malinovsky during the war, when the latter was an obscure prisoner in a German prison camp, demonstrates his conviction of the ex-Deputy's innocence of the spy charge. Lenin sent him reading matter and material for agitation among the other Russian prisoners. Krupskaya sent him food parcels, took care of his laundry and clothes and performed other services that had no political meaning beyond that of personal comradeship. Late in 1916 (two or three months before his exposure) the Bolshevik paper *Sotsial Demokrat* publicly stated that Malinovsky had been "fully rehabilitated" by his subsequent conduct, for his past crime of "desertion of his post."

> I did not believe [testified Citizen Ulyanov before the Extraordinary Investigating Commission of the Provisional Government] in provocateurship here, and for the following reason: If Malinovsky were a provocateur, the Okhrana would not gain from that as much as our Party did from *Pravda* and the whole legal apparatus. It is clear that by bringing a provocateur into the Duma and eliminating for that purpose all the competitors of bolshevism, etc., the Okhrana was guided by a gross conception of bolshevism, I should say rather a crude, homemade (*lubochnii*) caricature. They imagined that the Bolsheviks would arrange an armed insurrection. In order to keep all the threads of this coming insurrection in their hands, they thought it worth while to have recourse to all sorts of things to bring Malinovsky into the Duma and the Central Committee. But when the Okhrana succeeded in both these matters, what happened? It happened that Malinovsky was transformed into one of the links of the long and solid chain connecting our illegal base with the two chief legal organs by which our Party influenced the masses: *Pravada* and the Duma Fraction. The *agent provocateur* had to serve both these organs in order to justify his vocation.
>
> Both these organs were under our immediate guidance. Zinoviev and I wrote daily to *Pravda* and its policy was entirely determined by the resolution of the Party. Our influence over forty to sixty thousand workers was thus secured . . . [*Vestnik Vremmenago Pravitelstva*—News Bulletin of the Provisional Government, June 16, 1917, p. 3.]

As always, to Lenin a gain for the faction was equivalent to a gain for "our Party" and for "the revolution."

Whether he was right in calculating that the split in the Duma was a gain, or whether the police were right in thinking it a loss to the revolutionary movement, we must leave to the reader to decide as he considers the events of the year 1917. At any rate, the police were so convinced of the desirability of a split that the loss of Malinovsky's services and the simultaneous alarming news that the International Socialist Bureau was calling a new unity conference of all Russian factions caused the police chief to issue a general circular of instructions to all his subordinates and secret agents. Beletsky was no longer police head, and Assistant Minister Junkovsky was now the deciding force, yet the poltical line of the police remained the same. The circular read:

> Information received from political agents points to a tendency recently exhibited within the ranks of the Russian Social Democratic Party toward the unification of the different factions . . . In view of the exceptional gravity of this intention and the undesirability of its taking place, the Police Department considers it necessary to . . . impress upon their secret agents the necessity for participating in the various Party conferences, there to insist, firmly and convincingly, upon the utter impossibility of any such fusion, particularly the fusion of the Bolsheviki and the Mensheviki.

The last act in this strange drama of Roman Malinovsky occurred in November, 1918, when Lenin had been in power for a full year. On November 2, reckless adventurer to the end, Malinovsky crossed the Russian border and turned up in Petrograd. For three successive days he visited the Smolny Institute (Bolshevik headquarters), demanding either to be arrested or taken to see Lenin. On the third day, Zinoviev saw him and ordered his arrest. He was taken to Moscow for trial. The Bolshevik Krylenko, who was later to conduct many prosecutions until he himself disappeared in a purge, was appointed as prosecutor.

He knew the defendant well since he too had reason to believe that one of his arrests by the tsarist police was Malinovsky's work. The trial was swift and secret. But the workers' organizations of Moscow sent deputations to attend, for they feared that Lenin might exonerate their ex-Deputy once more.

Accounts of the trial are confused and sometimes deliberately confusing. But from Bolshevik memoirs, and the writings of Burtsev, we are able to reconstruct some scenes of this last act. A trick of fate put Burtsev in jail in the same cell as ex-Police Chief Beletsky, when the latter was testifying at Malinovsky's trial. Another important source was Malinovsky's old colleague, the Bolshevik Duma Deputy, Badaev. Where Badaev and Burtsev (in *Struggling Russia*, I, No. 9-10) agree, we are likely to be on firm ground.

Malinovsky's bearing at the trial was proud and challenging. He demanded that Lenin be summoned as a witness. According to some accounts, this was refused. But the Bolshevik Olga Anikst, in a memoir in Vol. IV of the series "About Lenin" published by the official Gosizdat (Moscow, 1925, p. 93), tells how she watched Lenin closely during the trial. All through it his head remained bowed, and he took notes. But when the defense counsel in his summary said that if Malinovsky had had friends to guide him properly, he would never have become a spy, Lenin looked up at Malinovsky and emphatically nodded his head. If so, it was his only testimony.

Malinovsky asserted that Lenin must have known of his role after his resignation from the Duma. He had further tried to tell Lenin that his past was "filled with abominations," but Lenin had refused to listen, saying that for Bolsheviks these personal misdeeds of his youth had no meaning. Did not Lenin know that the police had a hold on him? Still Lenin had permitted him to rehabilitate himself in a German prison camp, and the Bolshevik

organ, *Sotsial Demokrat*, in December, 1916, declared that
he had been "fully rehabilitated."

> The best period of my life was the two and one-
> half years which I devoted to propaganda among the
> Russian prisoners in Germany. I did a great deal dur-
> ing that time for the spread of the ideas of Bolshevism.
> [From Burtsev's article.]

And Badaev writes:

> He alleged that he was forced to become an *agent
> provocateur* because he was already completely in the
> hands of the police. He represented his career as a
> long martyrdom, accompanied by suffering and re-
> morse from which he could not escape . . . He tried
> to prove that he left the Duma of his own free will
> because of personal unhappiness, and that he ob-
> tained permission from the police to quit politics . . .
> He adopted a pose of sincere repentance while admit-
> ting the gravity of his crimes.

A notable procession of witnesses testified in the trial:
ex-Police Chief Beletsky; ex-Assistant Chief Vissarionov;
ex-Minister of the Interior Makarov; ex-Deputy Minister
Junkovsky; former Duma Deputies Badaev and Petrovsky;
and many of the Bolshevik men and women whom he had
betrayed to the police. Both Junkovsky and Beletsky were
asked leading questions to elicit "proof" that his activities
had benefited the Bolsheviks and "the Revolution" more
than the police. Beletsky agreed to this, but Junkovsky
answered with dignity that he was "an honest monarchist
and that he could not enter into a discussion of that question." (Account of Burtsev.)

How much did Lenin know of Malinovsky's past?
How well did he understand what manner of man he was
using in the German prison camps, in disregard of the
accusations of the Mensheviks, of Bukharin and Rozmirovich, and the scandal of his resignation from the Duma?

According to Gorky, Lenin said that he had been able to
see through Alexinsky, but not through Malinovsky. At
the first meeting with Alexinsky, Lenin said:

> "I had a feeling of physical repulsion to him. I
> couldn't conquer it . . . I had to use every method to
> keep myself in check . . . I simply couldn't stand this
> degenerate." Then, shrugging his shoulders in amaze-
> ment, he said: "But I never saw through that scoundrel
> Malinovsky. That was a very mysterious affair, Mali-
> novsky." (M. Gorky, *Lenin* Centrizdat, Moscow, 1931,
> pp. 45-46.)

It was indeed. And so, for all the memoirs and an-
alyses, it remains. Why did Lenin exonerate Malinovsky
in 1914, against the evidence and against the world? Why
did he rehabilitate him in 1916? Why did Malinovsky return to Russia when Lenin was in power? Did he count
on Lenin? Why did Lenin then not lift a finger to save
him?

Malinovsky's closing words at the trial, according to
Badaev, were a profession of sincere repentance and devotion to the Revolution, a reminder that he had returned
voluntarily to Bolshevik Russia.

And according to Burtsev:

> When the Revolution triumphed in Germany and
> Russia and the possibility of participating promi-
> nently in political activities was lost to him forever,
> he decided to go back and die, rather than to flee into
> the obscurity of an Argentina or a similar place of
> refuge. Of course, he could have committed suicide,
> but he preferred to die in the view of everybody, and
> had no fear of death.

The verdict was "death." Malinovsky was shot that
same night, shortly after the trial ended, at 2 o'clock in
the morning. Was there a special reason for the speed?

Until the archives of that period are opened, if they
still exist, the only certain verdict in the Malinovsky case

is the single sentence of Lenin to Gorky: "That was a very mysterious affair, Malinovsky . . ."

Even that sentence, in the course of Stalin's great *operation palimpsest*, vanished from subsequent editions of Gorky's memoirs. And the new writings on the palimpsest by Nikita Sergeevich Khrushchev and his successors have not restored it.

9

Trotsky: The History-Maker as Historian

LIKE THUCYDIDES, XENOPHON AND JOSEPHUS, Napoleon and Churchill, Leon Trotsky had to wait to write his major history until defeat had deprived him of the possibility of making history. But all his life he was a writer by avocation, and a history-maker by vocation. "Beginning in 1897," he wrote in his autobiography, "I have waged the fight chiefly with a pen in my hand."[1] When he was writing for *Iskra* he chose a nom de guerre—not to say nom de plume; it was *Pero*, the Russian word for *pen*.

Unlike Lenin, Trotsky looked often at himself in the mirror of history and consciously treasured his personal historic role. After 1905, in which year he played a more important part than any other revolutionary leader, he chose the first moment of respite, exile in Vienna, to write *Die Russische Revolution: 1905* (Vienna, 1908 and 1909). It is a book of 334 oversized octavo pages of social analysis, history, political polemics, personal narrative, and apologia. At present forbidden in Russia, out of print in Germany, and never published in English, it remains an

---

[1] Leon Trotsky, *My Life* (New York, 1930), p. viii.

extremely important source for the study of the 1905 revolution.

Leon Trotsky did not find time to woo the muse of history again until 1929 found him once more in exile from his native land, for the third and last time, on the Turkish island of Prinkipo. Then he wrote two works of major importance to the historian: his autobiography (1929), which of necessity contains much history; and his *History of the Russian Revolution* (Vol. I, 1930, Vols. II and III, 1932), which contains much autobiography, although he always refers to himself in the third person.

The first thing to note about Trotsky as historian is that we are dealing with a persuasive and frequently pedantic polemicist who was both a great orator and a great master of literary style. He is proud of the year 1917, telling of it as an old soldier reliving his greatest battles, for in it his role was huge, and his whole life until 1917 was dedicated to bringing about the seizure of power "by the proletariat," with which the year ends. If Lenin provided the party machine and the conspirative bent and concentration on power, it was Trotsky who provided the central doctrine[2] and the actual military-political strategy of the armed conquest of power. Trotsky's skillful and eloquent pen is here dedicated to the glorification of the Bolshevik seizure of power, the defense of his own role in it, and to the scorn, mockery, caricature, gross and cruel misrepresentation of all the defeated—a scorn that is more cruel when he deals with liberals, democrats, and the other socialist factions or parties than when he deals with the Tsar, the monarchists, or the reactionaries.

Decorativeness, metaphor, and verbal fireworks come

[2] The Mensheviks tended to sum up their aims in the formula "bourgeois democratic revolution"; Lenin's algebraic formula had been "democratic dictatorship of the proletariat and the peasantry"; "people's government" summarizes the immediate aim of the Socialist Revolutionaries; Trotsky's formula was "permanent revolution, beginning as a dictatorship of the working class and ending in world revolution."

naturally to Trotsky. Thus of Skobelev, formerly his follower and in 1917 a leader of the Executive Committee of
the Soviet, he writes: "He conveyed the impression of a
student playing the role of statesman on a home-made
stage." Of Chernov: "Abstention from voting became for
him a form of political life." Of Kerensky: "His strength
in the period of dual power lay in his combining the weaknesses of liberalism with the weaknesses of democracy."
Of the Tsar: "Nicholas inherited from his ancestors not only
a giant empire, but also a revolution. And they did not
bequeath him one quality which would have made him
capable of governing an empire . . . Or even a county."
Of the mob: "A revolution is always distinguished by im-
politeness, probably because the ruling classes did not take
the trouble in good season to teach the people fine manners." Of the Chairman of the Duma: "Rodzyanko tried
to put down the revolution with the aid of a fire hose: he
wept." Of the Provisional Government: "It sneaked on
tiptoe around the blaze of the revolution, choking from
the smoke, and saying to itself: let it burn down to the
embers, then we'll try to cook up something." Of the
socialists in the first coalition government: "Being obliged
to enter the government in the name of the interests of the
Entente front . . . the Socialists took upon themselves a
third of the power, and the whole of the war." Bernard
Shaw, himself no mean wielder of the snickersnee, wrote
of this history: "When Trotsky cuts off his opponent's head,
he holds it up to show that there are no brains in it."

As an orator in 1917, and still as an historian in the
1930's Trotsky's first aim was to inflame the passions of the
multitude, above all the passion of hatred. Not so much
hatred of the Old Regime, which he detested coldly, pedantically, almost dispassionately, and which in any case was
already dead and a mere ghost six weeks before Lenin returned to try to overthrow "the freest government in the
world," and ten weeks before Trotsky reached Russia.
Rather, it was to inflame hatred of liberals, democrats, lib-

eral socialists, democratic socialists, pacifists, defenders of
the new Russia and of that government which, unlike the
one Lenin and Trotsky would set up, had the grace to regard itself as merely pre-legitimate and to call itself "provisional."

As an orator Trotsky was most effective at those
moments in history when the normally passive and in-
choate mass of unorganized men and women were stirred
and shaken out of their habitual responses, and bewildered
and made desperate by the mounting chaos of war, breakdown, and revolution. Then Leon Trotsky was able to
move the mass chorus to the center of the stage, give it
a sense of its own importance, enormous though transitory
(in Trotsky's intentions and still more in Lenin's, the independent activity of the masses was meant to be transitory); then he could turn bewilderment and frustration
into credulity concerning easy solutions and into anger,
hatred, distrust, and scorn for all and sundry, except the
Bolsheviks.

One of Trotsky's favorite audiences and participants
in the mass scenes he staged were the sailors of Kronstadt.
Having been held down by the despotic procedures of
that tiny floating despotism, a battleship, they rose up
against all commands, all discipline, all government. They
rejected not only the Provisional Government but the
All-Russian Soviet as well, setting up their "independent
Soviet Republic." They jailed their officers without trial
in the same hell holes that had been used to discipline
them, and drowned or bloodily lynched many. "The most
hateful," Trotsky observes, "were shoved under the ice,"[3]
of course while still alive. "Bloody acts of retribution," he
adds sententiously, "were as inevitable as the recoil of a
gun."[4] Even when, for once, Trotsky tried to restrain the
hatred he was playing upon (they were about to lynch

[3] Leon Trotsky, *The History of the Russian Revolution*, trans. Max
Eastman (3 vols.; New York, 1932), I, 255.
[4] *Ibid.*, p. 256.

Chernov), he did not forget to employ flattery: "You have
come here, you red men of Kronstadt, as soon as you heard
of the danger threatening the revolution . . . Long live
Red Kronstadt, glory and pride of the revolution."[5] When
he stood on Anchor Square in Kronstadt, egging on the
sailors against the Provisional Government and the Executive Committee of the Soviet, he said: "I tell you heads
must roll, blood must flow. . . . The strength of the French
Revolution was in the machine that made the enemies of
the people shorter by a head. This is a fine device. We
must have it in every city."[6]

In 1921, Trotsky would direct picked troops headed
by delegates to a Bolshevik Congress across the ice to
reduce the "flower of the revolution" to submission, because they did not know when to stop self-activity and
anarchic opposition to dictatorial rule, but this episode
falls outside the scope of Trotsky's three volumes.

As a "Marxist" historian, Trotsky begins his work with
an economic picture, proceeding from that to class structure, class struggles, class parties, and a class analysis of
each action, speech, proposal, personage.

The economic picture begins with an account of
Russia's backwardness, which to Trotsky has enormous advantages. These are not the ones usually noted, namely,
that the later a country enters into industrialism the more
it finds to borrow from the latest techniques of other lands
without having to pass through the earlier stages and
without being saddled with many obsolete and obsolescent
plants. The advantages as Trotsky sees them are mainly
political, and give rise to his enunciation of what he regards
as the "fundamental law" of the Russian Revolution.

[5] The episode is in Trotsky's *History*, Vol. II. The words of Trotsky's
speech are recorded in N. N. Sukhanov, *The Russian Revolution: 1917*,
trans. Joel Carmichael (New York, 1955), p. 446. In Sukhanov's original
Zapiski o revoliutsii, the episode and words quoted are in Vol. IV, pp.
423-35.
[6] Wladimir Woytinsky, *Stormy Passage*, New York, 1961, p. 286.

First, the more backward the economy, the weaker will be the bourgeoisie and the more retarded the democratic structure, which Trotsky ties dogmatically to what he calls the "bourgeois democratic revolution." Hence when Russia borrows the techniques of modern heavy industry, it creates a proletariat that is more concentrated, more powerful, and of course, more revolutionary than the bourgeoisie. Hence Trotsky's slogan of "No tsar but a workers' government." The bourgeoisie is expendable, and along with it, the "democratic revolution" identified by him with its rule.

Second, the later in history a revolution occurs, the more "advanced" and "modern" is the ideology which it can import. Russia is overthrowing tsarism in the twentieth century, which—again dogmatically—is one century too late for a democratic revolution or a constituent assembly. "In the middle of the seventeenth century," Trotsky writes, "the bourgeois revolution in England developed under the guise of a religious reformation." In the eighteenth century, France was able to skip the Reformation. In the twentieth, after the flourishing of Marxist socialism, "just as France stepped over the Reformation, so Russia stepped over the formal democracy."[7]

The Soviet dictatorship is, by definition, the dictatorship of the proletariat. (Writing in 1930-32 Trotsky gives no sign that it has turned out to be the dictatorship of the party over all classes, including the workingmen, in the proletariat's name.) Hence it dispenses with "pure democracy" as the French Revolution did with "the Reformation." These propositions concerning "backwardness" and "borrowing" form the core of Trotsky's famous "law of combined development."

This "general law" leads to innumerable deductions, inferences, corollaries, and obiter dicta, of which the following is a typical example:

[7] Trotsky, *History*, I, 14-15.

> We may lay this down as a law: Revolutionary gov-
> ernments are the more liberal, the more tolerant, the
> more "magnanimous" to the reaction, the shallower
> their program, the more they are bound up with the
> past, the more conservative their rôle. And the con-
> verse: the more gigantic their tasks and the greater
> the number of vested rights and interests they are to
> destroy, the more concentrated will be the revolu-
> tionary power, the more naked its dictatorship.[8]

Such propositions are invariably treated as self-evident,
and are at hand to settle any question.

No less self-evident, and easy to manipulate dogmatically, does our historian find the concept of class. For
Trotsky it is an axiom that only one class must lead in a
twentieth-century revolution, and only one emerge from
it as the sole and necessarily dictatorial ruler: namely, the
proletariat. It is no less axiomatic that there is only one
party that is proletarian and socialist; all the rest are bourgeois, or—at once more gently and more scornfully—petty
bourgeois.

If a party believes that the people (narod) should
make the revolution and the people should rule, and that
narod includes both peasants and workers, and even intellectuals—as did the Socialist Revolutionary Party—that
party is petty bourgeois. Even if a party shares the same
program with the Bolsheviks, as the Mensheviks did between 1903 and 1919, that does not entitle it to the cachet
of proletarian or socialist. Those are accolades reserved
by history for the Bolsheviks, the party of Lenin and
Trotsky. This makes all political history beautifully simple.

Any resolution of the Soviet Executive, made up over-
whelmingly until October 1917 of Socialist Revolutionaries
and Mensheviks, with a Bolshevik minority, is automatically
a bourgeois decision, unless the Bolsheviks propose and
vote for it.

[8] *Ibid.*, p. 236.

The Moscow City Duma, elected by a vote that was 58 per cent Socialist Revolutionary, a little under 12 per cent Menshevik, and a few percentage points less Bolshevik, with about 17 per cent Constitutional Democrats and virtually no reactionaries, whenever it takes a decision against the vote of the Bolsheviks, is said to represent the bourgeoisie or the "pressure of bourgeois circles."

The war is equally uncomplicated. It is bourgeois imperialist by definition. Hence all who wish to continue it —even if they overthrow Miliukov for giving expression to "imperialist aims," if they try to force on the Allies and the Central Powers an early peace without victors or vanquished, if they are for self-determination for all peoples, even if they are merely in favor of defending revolutionary Russia against invasion, or for an early separate peace without further revolution in Russia and without world revolution—they are all bourgeois imperialist by definition.

The problems of power—of provisional government, dual power, soviet power, constituent assembly, democracy, and dictatorship—are solved just as easily and infallibly by the chanted formulae of this sorcerer's apprentice.[9] The Provisional Government is capitalist by definition. The dual power is a simultaneous rule by "two classes," the one "the bourgeoisie" grouped around the Provisional Government, and the other, that of "the workers and soldiers," grouped around the Soviet. That makes the Provisional Government, *ipso facto,* bourgeois. But if the Soviet does not take all power into its hands, and continues to support the Provisional Government, that makes the Soviet majority, its leadership, and its actions, bourgeois too. Or petty bourgeois. (The petty bourgeois seems to be one who is bourgeois by definition, without knowing it.)

What if the Soviet should take all power, the slogan around which the epic battle is waged throughout most

[9] The justification for this term will be found in the last sentence of this chapter.

of these three volumes? One would think that this must represent the triumph of the proletariat. But not so fast! The Soviets, from February through September, still have a democratic socialist, hence a petty bourgeois, majority. The seizure of all power by the Soviet would only transfer the battle for power to a more favorable battleground. Only when the Bolsheviks have won a majority will this organization of "workers and soldiers" become "proletarian." And then its proletarian transfiguration will be automatic. "Only the guiding layers" (he means thereby the Bolshevik Party) "have a political program. . . . Without a guiding organization the energy of the masses would dissipate like steam which is not enclosed in a piston-box."[10]

Clearly the Constituent Assembly is no proper piston box or piston for the steam of the locomotive of history. This, too, is clear by definition, for the Constituent Assembly is nineteenth century; it represents "pure" or "formal" democracy; it gives representation to the nation, the whole people, that is, all classes of the population. Hence it cannot serve twentieth-century socialism nor the proletarian dictatorship nor the rule of the "guiding layers." Any who in 1917 work for the fulfillment of the century-old dream that the Russian people should at long last determine their own destiny in freedom and write for themselves a charter of public liberties and social reforms, are fit only to be condemned as at best petty bourgeois, to be cast aside, and, in the end, denied the freedom to form a party or voice a program. Those who urge that land committees prepare a fair and systematic transfer of the land to the peasants, but want to wait for the completion of the program and its ratification by the Constituent Assembly, are caught in the same net of annihilation by labels.

It is true that on the eve of the seizure of power, when Trotsky delivered his presidential address on his election to the presidency of the Petrograd Soviet, he

[10] Trotsky, *History*, I, xviii-xix.

solemnly pledged: "We shall conduct the work of the Petrograd Soviet in a spirit of lawfulness and of full freedom for all parties. The hand of the Presidium will never lend itself to the suppression of the minority."[11]

But as historian, Trotsky prefers to forget this pledge. This is one time he neglects to record the unforgettable words of Leon Trotsky. When Sukhanov, three years after the Bolshevik seizure of power, reminded him of the pledge, he lapsed into silence for a while, then said wistfully: "Those were good days."[12]

I cannot close this all too brief analysis of these three stout volumes without at least a word on what the historian will find in them.

First, there is a powerful and eloquent statement of the doctrines and dogmas that guided Lenin and Trotsky in 1917.

Second, there are brilliant word pictures of scenes of revolution and masses in action.

Third, there are remarkable profiles, one-sided and unfair to the point of caricature, but always vivid and revealing, of all the principle actors.

Fourth, there is an account, unparalleled in historical literature, of the strategy and tactics, the military moves, in the preparation of the deceptive conspiracy of October to seize power under the guise of merely defending the revolution. Trotsky exults in his skill in disguising every step in the offensive as a defensive action, and enjoys now his recollection and meticulous exposition after the events of all the details which he knew better than any other man, even Lenin; for it was he, as Chairman of the Military Revolutionary Committee and Petrograd Soviet, who plotted every step, wrapped each maneuver in the brazen impudence of his eloquence, and personally directed the fulfillment of each measure. The chapters on the "Military

11 Sukhanov, *Zapiski* . . . , VI, 188ff.
12 *Ibid.*, p. 190.

Revolutionary Committee" and on the "Conquest of the Capital" are not equaled by all the other literature on the event put together.

Fifth, this history lays bare, both where it intends and where it does not intend, the soul of one of the principal actors in the October seizure of power—at the brief moment of consummation, the most important actor.

Finally, it is a history which no historian of Russia and no historian of revolution can afford to neglect. But let him be forewarned that Trotsky's is a pen that is frequently as persuasive as it is continuously one-sided. It is always the historian's duty, too often neglected out of worship of the bitch-goddess Success, to seek out the truths of the defeated along with the truths that get published by the victors. But particularly here must the reader come well equipped with an awareness of the truths of the defeated—the more so because somewhere concealed in this blinding flood of words which record the victory of Trotsky and his party, are also some of the secrets which explain why Trotsky, too, must in the end be reckoned as one of the defeated.

10

The
Strange Case
of
Litvinov's Diary

SOMETIME IN 1952 or early 1953, Gregory Bessedovsky, a former Soviet diplomat resident in Paris, approached officials of various governments and representatives of publishing houses with a manuscript purporting to be the diary of Maxim Litvinov, who had died in 1951. At the suggestion of a high official of the British Foreign Office, a British publisher, André Deutsch, asked the historian Edward Hallett Carr to investigate the manuscript's authenticity. After reading the Russian typescript, Professor Carr encouraged Deutsch to go ahead with the book, and undertook to go to Paris himself for further checking. There he picked up the following trail: Gregory Bessedovsky, the man offering the manuscript for sale, said he had gotten it from a Mr. X, a Russian businessman in Paris ("politically colorless"), who had gotten it from a Mr. Y resident in Stockholm, who had gotten it from the late Alexandra Kollontay, then Russian Ambassador to Sweden, who had gotten it from Litvinov himself. Mr. X proved of no interest; Mr. Y refused to come to Paris or to meet Professor Carr in Stockholm, but consented to answer written questions "given to Bessedovsky."

Professor Carr wrote an interim report giving it as his conclusion that the manuscript "has a *prima facie* claim to be regarded as authentic, and a serious historical document." If Mr. Y should answer his written questions satisfactorily, Carr declared, he would be willing to write a signed introduction and supply notes. If not, he still thought the diary should be published, would give Deutsch help and advice, but would withhold the use of his name. Carr received satisfactory answers, wrote an introduction and footnotes.

It was at this point that the writer of these lines was brought into the affair by an American publisher as Professor Carr had been brought in by the British house. The publisher, Harper and Brothers (now Harper and Row), received a microfilm of the Russian typescript, a history of the manuscript thus far, and a copy of the Carr interim report.

The microfilm showed one hundred sheets typewritten in Russian, with not a single alteration or correction in handwriting. At one point there did appear, however, a hand-drawn Chinese character, of which more later. The entries were scrappy and disjointed. Many were fragments of sentences ending with three dots. Some entries bore a date, usually only a year, or a year and one or more months. Page 1 of the microfilm began with what is now the second entry in the book; the first entry was somehow added later. The microfilm began with "May-June, 1926" and ended vaguely in 1936, forming about three-quarters of the book as it now appears.[1] I was subsequently to learn that this same 100-frame microfilm had been sold earlier to a government official as the "complete diary."

I had long known that Litvinov was secretly alienated from Stalin by the blood purges of the nineteen-thirties,

---

[1] *Notes for a Journal*, by Maxim Litvinov. Introduction by E. H. Carr. London: André Deutsch, 303 pp. American edition, Introduction by E. H. Carr and Prefatory Note by General Walter Bedell Smith. William Morrow, 347 pp. Harper decided not to publish for reasons which will appear below.

which had claimed all his chief assistants and intimates in the Soviet Foreign Office and its embassies, and only narrowly missed Litvinov himself. Another diplomat whom I knew to be deeply disaffected had been Alexandra Kollontay. At the end of World War II, Litvinov had tried to hint to one of our high officials that America was engaging in dangerous appeasement of Soviet demands which might later lead to another war. When the official failed to take the hint, Litvinov had braved death to call in Richard C. Hottelet, one of our most respected journalists and commentators, and using scarcely veiled "Aesopian language," he had made the warning more explicit. I knew that Hottelet had told American diplomatic officers, but had honorably refrained from publishing his "scoop," until natural death, that most unnatural of deaths for an Old Bolshevik, had put Litvinov out of danger. With this background in mind, I approached the diary with eagerness and a predisposition to believe in its authenticity.

The opening pages were not reassuring. They began with the first of a series of visits from a rabbi named Schechtman, who comes to Litvinov as one Jew to another to complain that the League of the Godless had looted two synagogues and arrested the rabbi of Kiev on charges of currency speculation. Litvinov promises to intervene, although he knows that "Koba [Stalin] doesn't like me to interfere in questions concerning the Jewish religion." The last time Litvinov had tried to help non- or anti-Bolshevik Jews, Stalin "threatened to bring the matter to the attention of the Central Control Commission. . . . I couldn't help smiling at the threat; Soltz, the head of the C.C.C., is the son of the rabbi of Vilna."

Thus the opening passage presented Litvinov as a philo-Semitic Jew, ready to defend any and every Jew against his government and his party. The same un-communist Jewish solidarity is attributed to the fanatical head of the Central Control Commission, Soltz. Actually, both

Litvinov and Soltz had rejected their Jewish heritage in their youth. Their Jewish origin tended to make them more rather than less hostile toward religious and anti-communist Jews. But such passages, in which all Jews in the communist camp are portrayed as holding with each other and with non- and anti-communist Jews against the party, are scattered through the diary. The Jewish Kaganovich gives it as his opinion that "all Jewish members of the party should be Trotsky's declared and convinced enemies." In the late twenties Litvinov is portrayed as getting interested (because "as a Jew he had no right to refuse assistance") in protecting Zionists in Russia from persecution, arrest, and deportation to Siberia. In actual fact, Zionism was outlawed as early as 1919, and all known Zionists were either dead or in Siberia before the diary opens. I realized that I was dealing with something which I have frequently met in French boulevard "revelations": the "international Jewish conspiracy," the myth of a Jewish solidarity overriding all political and other differences.

I opened my report to the American publisher with this observation. He in turn sent it to the British publisher, who may or may not have forwarded it to Bessedovsky and Carr. At any rate, when the book appeared, none of these passages was excised, but the first journal entry on Schechtman had mysteriously become the second journal entry. Professor Carr, who writes that the "problem of authenticity was further complicated after my return to London by the receipt of another instalment . . . the whole section from 1937 onward," has nothing to say about a new first entry, except to observe that "the conversation with Trotsky and Yoffe in 1926 with which the Journal opens . . . shows an intimate knowledge of party affairs."

Without stopping to check, I read the microfilm through from end to end, but could not find so much as a line that was in Litvinov's style. To be sure, he was never much of a writer or theoretician, but we have from his pen and tongue a multitude of speeches, prepared and extempore, interviews with the press, articles, pamphlets, reminiscences, memoranda, diplomatic and semi-diplomatic notes, open letters, political letters, purely personal letters. The style in all of these is distinguished by directness, simplicity bordering on artlessness, frankness and explicitness insofar as creed, overriding instructions, and special pleading permitted. And always there was a sort of workman-like clarity. Not a line in all these hundred microfilm pages (or in the material which bobbed up later), not even by imitation or accident, was in Maxim Litvinov's public or private style. Not a hint of his showmanship and public triumphs at Geneva, in Washington, or at the League of Nations. Litvinov once remarked: "The idea of collective security, the formulation, 'peace is indivisible,' and the definition of aggression and the aggressor, are perhaps my contribution to the abstract science of peace." When he advanced these "contributions" they were part of the fraudulent peace campaigns of the Soviet Union, but that he had increasingly come to believe in them as his contribution to his country and his time is proved by his hazardous interview with Richard Hottelet. With false pathos, as the diary draws to a close, its author writes: "All my life is in these notes . . . And my work . . . Some day history will pass its judgment . . ."[2] Yet there is nothing in the diary of that which Litvinov had come to feel was his life's real contribution.

In his introduction, Professor Carr suggests that the "conspicuous incoherence of the document, and the abrupt changes of mood and style, are perhaps an argument in its favor." "It is difficult," he adds, "to avoid the hypothesis that at least two hands have been at work on the document." But the question remains whether there is any reason for believing that either of these hands was Litvinov's. If style is the man, then somewhere, either by

---

[2] The three dots (. . .) do not represent omissions by the present writer, but are in the microfilm and text as published.

studied imitation or by accident, the man Litvinov should appear in these pages.

Then whose hand, or hands, had written it? Whose style or touch might be recognized? Available to me were the same clues as were available to Professor Carr, except that I could not interview Bessedovsky or Mr. X, or write to Mr. Y. So the search led me to a study of the writings of Gregory Bessedovsky, who had left the service of the Soviets some twenty-five years before.

I began with the peculiar fact that on page 11 of the microfilm, the diarist had taken the trouble to draw a Chinese ideograph. Litvinov knew no Chinese; drawing or brushing in ideographs is a complicated business—more incredible is it still to remember a single ideograph's form from the year 1926 to the time when the diary was dictated or typed. According to the diary, Karakhan, Soviet Ambassador to China, was ignorant of Chinese despite his vainglorious pretensions to the contrary. Mao Tse-tung is pictured as having been in Moscow in 1926 (there is ample proof that he was not) in order to consult with Russian leaders. He delivers an address in halting Russian, and when he gets stuck, draws a Chinese ideograph to represent the word "eloquence," whereupon Karakhan volunteers the translation "wooden mouth."[3]

On page 141 of Bessedovsky's *Revelations of a Soviet Diplomat* (London, 1931), the author writes that during the year 1927 while he was in Japan he studied the Japanese language. Japanese has the same written characters as Chinese. "Every day I learned a half dozen hieroglyphs." On page 149, he tells how he made a laughable mistake owing to a confusion of ideographs, which led him to address a prince as "your imperial electricity" when he meant to say "your imperial highness." This was the clue

[3] The ideograph itself has been omitted from the published version of *Notes for a Journal*, but the reference to it can be found on pages 36-37.

I was looking for, and it led me to additional discoveries, of which I cite only a few:

1. On pages 42-43 Litvinov makes an estimate of the Soviet diplomat Dogalevsky. The passage is an adaptation of page 163 of Bessedovsky.

2. On page 42, Litvinov notes the "filthy habits (now translated "bad habits") of his chief Chicherin, who works all night, plays piano at every hour of the day or night, makes Litvinov come to see him at two in the morning, and is then playing Chopin. It is highly improbable that as late as May, 1926, Litvinov would have noted Chicherin's habits in one of his first diary entries, for he would have been familiar with them for years, as was everyone who dealt with Chicherin.[4] But it is less unnatural that Bessedovsky should mention them in his first reference to Chicherin, whose habits he knew only from gossip. Actually pages 16-17 of the *Journal* are an adaptation of Bessedovsky, pages 93-95. Moreover, the diary has Litvinov say: "Chopin is his favorite, and he has no use for any other composer. . . ." The real Litvinov would have known that Chicherin's favorite composer was Mozart.

3. There is a peculiarly disproportionate amount of attention given to trivial scandals in a few of the world's capitals, almost always heard about from a third party, just as some minor official in any foreign service might have heard about them. Certain capitals are the subject of frequent allusions and detailed gossip, while others, no less important, are never even mentioned. Places that unaccountably attracted the diarist's interest for a certain period abruptly stop being referred to. For a space there are trivia from Warsaw, where Bessedovsky held a minor post in the Russian embassy from September 1923 to October 1925. The dates of the reports Litvinov receives from and about "Viktor" (Viktor Kopp) in Japan coincide

[4] In 1924 when I was in Moscow, Chicherin expressed a desire to talk with me, and when I asked his messenger to set a time and place he named the Foreign Office at 2 A.M.

with those of Bessedovsky's own year there, and the material resembles pages 131-35 and 137-40 of Bessedovsky's book. Litvinov receives news from Harbin that danger threatens Soviet possession of the Chinese-Eastern railway. Bessedovsky's book reveals that he was in Harbin at the end of 1927 "to see what was happening in the territory of the Chinese-Eastern railroad, and to have some conversations with its Soviet staff."

4. Before his defection Bessedovsky spent some time in the Soviet embassy in Paris under Dogalevsky. The details on Dogalevsky's life, appearance, and ways as given in the diary, of Rakovsky's difficulties in Paris, the circumstances of his recall, and all the revelations about the "Athenian nights," the "orgies" and the moral lapses of Soviet officials in Paris are closely paralleled in Bessedovsky's book. By a suggestive coincidence, Litvinov's interest in this or another foreign capital and his knowledge of the underworld aspects of Soviet diplomatic life there and of the life of that capital's statesmen coincide in point of time with Bessedovsky's stay in that place, and seem to fade when Bessedovsky moves on. After Bessedovsky's break with the Soviet Foreign Office, the diary, to quote Professor Carr on the later pages, "becomes markedly inferior in interest."

5. In various parts of the diary there is talk of the Soviet Ambassador to Japan, Viktor Kopp, of a quarrel about moral derelictions, and the need to recall Kopp. This is a reworking of Bessedovsky, pages 131-35. But at this point, Litvinov's otherwise perfect memory for names fails him. Writes Litvinov: "To Tokyo has been appointed a quite young worker from the Ukraine, a member of the Ukrainian Central Executive. What a strange idea to send as a diplomat to Japan a Ukrainian." I looked up the name of the Ukrainian. It was—Gregory Bessedovsky!

6. The diary is unusually tireless in its repeating of first name and patronymic every time a personage is mentioned. With Jews the diarist observes a special procedure

which is totally un-Russian, setting down only their pat-
ronymics without their first names: thus Lev Davidovich
Trotsky is called Davidovich, and Adolph Abramovich
Yoffe is called Abramovich. Unlike other diarists, Litvinov
does not resort to initials even on the tenth mention of
a name, but on page 68, there is another singular failure
to give a name at all: "The new *chargé d'affaires* to Paris
received instructions directly from Koba. That is monstrous. . . ." The name of the *chargé d' affaires* turns out to
be Bessedovsky! He tells his story of his direct interview
with Koba-Stalin on pages 190-92 of his own book.

This coyness about the name of Bessedovsky seems
to be contagious. In his interim report, Professor Carr
wrote to André Deutsch, "I have had two long meetings
with Bessedovsky." But in his introduction to the book,
Professor Carr writes: "I visited Paris—in an attempt to
obtain detailed and accurate information about the manuscript's provenance. According to statements made to me.
. . ." The name of Bessedovsky has again disappeared!
Since in the supposed chain of "provenance" whereby the
manuscript of the dairy reached the publisher's hand there
are only three people whose real names are given, and since
two of them, Litvinov and Kollontay, were dead, one
would have expected Carr at least to put the reader on
notice that a man named Bessedovsky had played the key
role in the transmission of the manuscript, and in vouching
for its authenticity. More particularly since Bessedovsky
had been the agent for another dubious manuscript, *My
Uncle Joseph Stalin*, by Budu Svanidze, the foreword to
whose American and British editions was written by him.
In that foreword Bessedovsky vouched for the identity
of Budu Svanidze and the authenticity of his book, but
Boris Souvarine, the French expert on communism, was
able to show that Budu Svanidze had never existed.[5]

To make matters still worse, Professor Carr a few

[5] See *Bulletin de l'Association d'Etudes et d'Informations Politiques
Internationales,* May 1953, Nos. 88 and 89.

pages later (page 14) actually uses the Russian edition
of Bessedovsky's own memoirs, from which I have been
quoting, to demonstrate the truthfulness of a dubious passage in the diaries! Professor Carr has been less than
candid with his readers—to put it mildly—in concealing the
chief name in the chain of "provenance" of the supposed
Litvinov diary, but when he uses Bessedovsky's own book
to silence doubts that may be aroused in the reader's mind
by a passage the diary contains on Benes, I prefer not to try
to qualify his procedure.

If in every line of the *Journal* there are things which
the real Litvinov could not have thought or said, on every
page there are absurdities and tokens of an ignorance which
a man so highly placed as he could not have been guilty
of. Professor Carr cites a few of these boners to suggest
that "at least two hands" composed the diary, but he by
no means cites the most ridiculous and impossible of them.
Here we shall have to content ourselves with a random
sampling.

There is Zoya Mossina, to whom more space is devoted
than to Roosevelt, Bullitt, Hull, Welles, Herriot, Blum,
and all the other statesmen Litvinov knew, put together.
A character straight out of a scandal sheet, she is represented as the secretary of the communist cell in the Soviet
Commissariat of Foreign Relations. On page 44 she has
the cell compel Litvinov to give classes in English to the
members of the Foreign Office. On page 46-47, Yagoda,
the dreaded head of the secret police, orders the hair-
dresser's shop in the Foreign Commissariat to close because
people talk too much in barber chairs, and there may be
leaks. Mossina gets Stalin to overrule Yagoda to protect
"socialist competition among the hairdressers." On pages
152ff. Zoya is running for re-election. There is a real campaign, balloting, stuffed ballot boxes, etc., etc. Placards
on the wall accuse Zoya of "encouraging abortions." The
Politburo tries to defeat her, but she gets re-elected any-
how. Molotov intervenes, and finally Stalin, who sends

Zoya off to a concentration camp. Stalin's wife, Alliluyeva, who, it is suggested on pages 169-70, seems to be having a Lesbian affair with Zoya, tries to get her out, and failing, commits suicide.

This is a fair picture of the level of most of the inside historical information in the diary. Kalinin impresses Ambassador Davies with his homespun quality (". . . he was priceless . . . he even picked his nose to show his peasant origins"). A foreign ambassador is seduced by ballerinas who are Cheka operatives and "Yezhov [chief of the secret police] listens in himself (through a bedroom microphone) —the ambassador yelps like a rabbit when he enjoys himself with our ballerinas. . . . so far the only case of collaboration of the NKVD and the capitalist world. . . ." Top party leaders who are about to be "confessed" and purged are brought to Yezhov's office with their wives, who are undressed and when naked are threatened with rape by Yezhov's special agent for raping, an ugly, hunchbacked, and syphilitic giant. They are softened by a sample raping, in the presence of Yezhov and his victims, of the eighteen-year-old daughter of one of the arrested party leaders. Bubnov has his son baptized, and Kaganovich has his circumcised. Litvinov was always opposed to the split between Bolsheviks and Social Democrats and there would have been world socialist unity had it not been for the "fanaticism of his [Lenin's] crazy scrap with Adler, Kautsky, Renner, Renaudel." (This "scrap," as both the author of the diary and the historian who introduces it could have ascertained, was about the proper socialist attitude toward World War I, and Litvinov himself wrote letters and reports boasting of his role in bringing about the split at a wartime conference he attended as Lenin's emissary.)

The most deplorable feature of this compendium of trivia, absurdity, and salacious backstairs gossip is that it is solemnly provided with all the externals of scholarship: an introduction by a historian of repute, appendices,

a bibliography of Litvinov's works, and innumerable footnotes. Typical of the use of these last is the following
passage from the body of the text.

"Koba has a new passion: the sister. . . . There are
rumors about young . . . [who shares this new passion's
sexual favors with Koba]. If Koba found out there would
be a tragedy. He is temperamentally unable to share anything. . . . Budyenny was simply a drunken n.c.o. when
he killed his wife. . . . Koba is different. . . . If Alliluyeva
keeps up her scenes in public he may. . . ."

Here a footnote re Budyenny is appended: "Budyenny, Semen Mikhailovich, Marshal, leading Soviet cav-
alry expert, Commissar for Defence in 1940."

Again we learn that "Koba's liaison with the actress
was broken off after he had been told of her amorous
adventures in Tiflis with Kinkhadze." To which a footnote is appended: "Kinkhadze. Chief of Georgian heavy
industry, then Foreign Minister of Georgia." When Litvinov is rusticated, he describes his wooden house as
having a cock on the roof, to which is appended the footnote: "Cock on the Roof. Common form of decoration on
peasant houses in Russia. Originates from an old super-
stition that the cock chases away evil spirits." Such are
the uses of scholarship.

There are three questions of real importance touched
on in the diary: the purges of the 1930's, the Chinese
Revolution, and the secret relations the Red Army had
with the Reichswehr before Hitler.

About the purges Litvinov knows nothing. He hears
gossip from third parties, gets the dates of trials and execu-
tions wrong, worries about the Jews among the victims,
and the possible rape of his daughter by the NKVD's rape
specialist. His diary tells us much less than any hitherto
published account, and what it does tell is trivial and
poverty-stricken invention.

On the Reichswehr, about which Litvinov could have

told much that is still secret, we get an absurd debate with himself as to whether to "withdraw" General Freiherr Kurt von Hammerstein from active service in Germany because "we need a military adviser in Mongolia. We will pay him in tsarist style even though we are Bolsheviks. We will satisfy the imperial Reichsofficer." Actually, at that moment Hammerstein was nothing less than Chief of Staff of the Third Command of the German Army. A little later he was made Deputy Chief of Staff of the entire Reichswehr. Even if he were a secret agent, is it likely that Russia would have withdrawn him from *that* key position? And even if he were paid "in tsarist style," it is hard to picture Hammerstein giving up such a post to go to Mongolia.

On the Chinese Revolution, all the dates are wrong, often by several years. All the Chinese leaders in the public eye today are made top men back in 1926-27 when in actual fact they were mere underlings; and everything is drowned in the usual brew of silly gossip. I have documented this elsewhere and will limit myself here to one major bit of "inside" misinformation.

As the diary opens, on "the third Saturday in May" of 1926 (one of the few exact dates given in the entire book), the Russians are conferring in Moscow with Mao Tse-tung, Chu Teh, and Li Ta-chao on how "to get rid of Chiang Kai-shek either physically or politically." Here we have a whole crowded nest of anachronisms. Mao Tse-tung, though already a second-string communist, was still a minor Kuomintang official in Yunnan; his association with Chu Teh was still several years away; all three of them were outranked by many Chinese communist leaders later to be purged; we know the real names of the Chinese leaders who were in Moscow for consultation in 1926. Chu Teh was there, but Mao was not. More important, Chiang Kai-shek was then Moscow-backed, and the hope of all the Russian communist leaders. His armies did not yet control all China, but held only one province out of eighteen. The chief Soviet concern was to back him to the limit in order to enable him to begin what was to become his famous sweep to the north. Litvinov pictures Stalin as wanting to destroy Chiang at that time, although he controlled only one out of China's eighteen provinces, because Stalin had to assume a "false revolutionary pose" under the pressure of "attacks by Radek and Trotsky."

Actually, we have two speeches on the "Chinese question" by Stalin in 1926, and they contain no hint of his future " revolutionary pose." He rebukes a young disciple named Mif, not an oppositionist, for proposing Soviets for the Chinese peasants, and he calls for "support of the Canton Army, inspired by an idea, the idea of the struggle against imperialism, heartened by the passion which will bring about the emancipation of China" and overwhelm "the counter-revolutionary Northern armies." Finally, there was no disagreement or opposition criticism for another year on this score, so that in 1927 Stalin could remind his critics that "you too supported and were in full agreement with this tactic and your criticism is an afterthought."

Professor Carr tells us that if this diary is a forgery, its "motive is commercial, not political . . . the author appears as in many respects ambivalent in his judgments, and in particular in his attitude to Stalin. This gives the document, whether genuine or not, a certain value for the historian."

The first purpose of the forgery mill for "inside" books on Russia that has its headquarters in France and branches in England, Germany, the United States, and perhaps other countries, is undoubtedly to make money. When we total up the number of first serializations, and publications in France, England, Germany, more rarely in the United States, Italy, and Latin America, and the substantial sums paid by American magazines for options which, after investigation, they generally do not exercise, I am convinced that the industry is profitable. But I fail to comprehend why a forgery is any more valuable to the historian because its motive is profit, and its forged passages, whether through laziness or design, are "ambivalent."

Actually, the forgeries have a political function too, though that is harder to pin down. On the surface, all these "revelations" designed to fill the vacuum left by Soviet secrecy appear to be anti-Soviet. They are that in a vulgar, prurient, scandal-sheet fashion: full of orgies, lechery, deeds of sadistic cruelty, international Jewish conspiracies, and evidence that the Soviet leadership need not be taken seriously. But virtually all this material, and the Litvinov "diary" no less than the other items, serves a directly opposite aim when it comes to certain large issues. The real cruelties and orgies always concern subordinates, particularly those already dead, whereas, despite a certain capriciousness, Stalin turns out to be a tower of strength, a man of foresight, a good father, a good Georgian, husband, or uncle, a simple lover of Georgian foods, wines, songs, a man who knows the masses as no other Soviet leader, and the possessor of various other average citizen's qualities which tend to normalize and humanize the total state and its late dictator. All the great black mysteries of his life are cleared up. Rudzutak is purged for moral reasons; Stalin does not know just whom Yezhov is to arrest next and even Stalin has to give in to him; Stalin shows concern for Piatakov in his illness and sends him honey, so that if Piatakov was purged there must have been good reason; Benes really deserved his fate at the time of the communist coup in Czechoslovakia, since he himself wrote a letter, "unfortunately proved genuine," which showed that he was "anti-Soviet," for in it he "claimed that he could bring about a coup d'état in Moscow"; the Soviet generals really did plot to betray Russia to Hitler, and it is suggested that their purge, which the diary places in the wrong year, headed off a military coup; Rosengolts confesses to Litvinov his own, Smilga's, and Piatakov's guilt; the Stalin-Hitler pact is justified in a half dozen separate places, although the "ambivalent" Litvinov was dead against it; in fact his "ambivalence" always ends with his testifying that Stalin was much wiser than he; in short, "this man has nerves of steel . . . is what our country and our age need . . . is a cynic but his knowledge of the masses is undeniable . . . is wiser than us all . . . slept under the same roof with the people whom Ilyich idealized . . . knows what is good for them . . . and for Russia."

The third, and to my way of thinking, most important role played by this species of literature, at least in France, where it is a booming business, is that by a sort of literary and historical Gresham's Law, these spicy, disjointed, bemusing concoctions tend to drive out of circulation truly serious studies on the nature of the Soviet system. Statesmen who will not labor to master Stalin's *Mein Kampf* any more than they did Hitler's, take Litvinov's "diaries" on their airplane journeys to conferences with the Russians and recommend them to subordinates as a means of understanding the real nature of the Soviet system. This sort of thing is easier to write than serious Soviet studies— and easier to read. Professor Carr finds the present volume "the most sensational of its kind yet published." He feels that it "makes a useful contribution to our understanding of the conditions in which Soviet policy was framed and conducted in these years and of the attitude of those concerned." The answer to this is best put in the words of the historian who reviewed the book for the *Times Literary Supplement* of September 9, 1955: "This book adds to our understanding of Soviet affairs and of Litvinov's personality about as much as a forged banknote adds to our wealth."

954

Also available from
STEIN AND DAY

THE FABULOUS LIFE OF DIEGO RIVERA
by Bertram D. Wolfe

STALIN: *An Appraisal of the Man
and His Influence* (new edition)
by Leon Trotsky
Edited and Translated by Charles Malamuth
Introduction by Bertram D. Wolfe

AN IDEOLOGY IN POWER:
Reflections on the Russian Revolution
by Bertram D. Wolfe

A LIFE IN TWO CENTURIES:
The Autobiography of Bertram D. Wolfe
by Bertram D. Wolfe

TROTSKY: *Fate of a Revolutionary*
by Robert Wistrich

KHRUSHCHEV
by Mark Frankland

SOLZHENITSYN
by David Burg and George Feifer

CHE GUEVARA: *A Biography*
by Daniel James

THE COMPLETE BOLIVIAN DIARIES OF CHE GUEVARA
AND OTHER CAPTURED DOCUMENTS
Edited and with an Introduction by Daniel James

POLITICIANS, SOCIALISM AND HISTORIANS
by A.J.P. Taylor

MAO TSE-TUNG: *The Man and the Myth*
by Eric Chou